Your Own Infinity

© 2019 Hargopal Kaur Khalsa

Published by the Kundalini Research Institute

PO Box 1819
Santa Cruz, NM 87532
www.kundaliniresearchinstitute.org

978-0-9786989-9-7

Compiled by: Hargopal Kaur Khalsa
Line Editor: Shanti Kaur Khalsa
Consulting Editor: Nirvair Singh Khalsa
Illustrations: Katie Yost
KRI Review: Siri Neel Kaur Khalsa
Design & Layout: PranaProjects, Ditta Khalsa & Biljana Nedelkovska

The diet, exercise and lifestyle suggestions in this book come from ancient yogic traditions. Nothing in this book should be construed as medical advice. Any recipes mentioned herein may contain potent herbs, botanicals and naturally occurring ingredients which have traditionally been used to support the structure and function of the human body. Always check with your personal physician or licensed health care practitioner before making any significant modification in your diet or lifestyle, to insure that the ingredients or lifestyle changes are appropriate for your personal health condition and consistent with any medication you may be taking. For more information about Kundalini Yoga as taught by Yogi Bhajan® please see www.yogibhajan.org and www.kundaliniresearchinstitute.org.

Table of Contents

KRIYAS & MEDITATIONS

JAPA

Dedication

To Yogi Bhajan, who lifted us up and gave us technology to lift ourselves when life felt like a burden, who pushed us when we thought we couldn't go any further, who helped us discover that many beliefs were nonsense, and who showed us ourselves when we were afraid to look. My prayer is that, with this sharing of his words, he serves you and future generations as well.

Introduction

In virtually every lecture, Yogi Bhajan steered us to God, to the Infinite, and to ourselves. Sometimes, he dropped a pearl of wisdom that shattered our misconceptions, our preconceptions, and exposed our astounding lack of perception. He found the angles that could penetrate our consciousness and clear a path to awareness.

There is a thirst to "know the unknown," to connect with the Divine, to experience Infinity, and to be the highest-consciousness being possible. Living in Los Angeles, where Yogi Bhajan lived for many years, gave me the opportunity to take classes with him. I must admit that, while the classes were incredible and I experienced vast states of consciousness, if you had asked me after class what Yogiji talked about, I would have been at a loss for words. Researching this book gave me the opportunity to delve into Yogi Bhajan's teachings, which are now online thanks to the Kundalini Research Institute, in the Yogi Bhajan Library of Teachings® (libraryofteachings.com). I listened to audio, watched videos, and read transcripts. Those passages that touched me, the ones I wanted deeply ingrained, are shared in this book.

The words in this book are all authentic quotes from Yogi Bhajan, edited only for grammar. I have provided the date of each lecture so that you can read more in the Library of Teachings.

The theme of this book took shape as I accumulated several pages of quotes. All along, it was clear that this book would not do justice to his teachings, because Yogi Bhajan spoke on such a vast array of topics. So, please excuse any omission of topics. Perhaps this compilation of quotes will inspire you to research a different subject. Take a deep dive into the Library of Teachings and witness how you incorporate his incandescent wisdom.

Who Is Yogi Bhajan

Harbhajan Singh Puri was born on August 26, 1929 in an area of India that is now Pakistan. He became a master of Kundalini Yoga at the age of sixteen, and he came to affectionately be known as Yogi Bhajan. He was the Mahan Tantric, of which there is only one at any time on the planet. He was an international religious leader with the official title of Siri Singh Sahib Bhai Sahib Harbhajan Singh Khalsa Yogiji.

While most spiritual teachers gather disciples, Yogi Bhajan came to Canada and then America to create teachers. He authored of over 50 books and inspired many more. He went on to start a successful and effective drug rehabilitation program called Superhealth®. Here are some quotes from Yogi Bhajan to give you a better introduction to our revered teacher in his own words:

Master of Kundalini Yoga

I became a master of Kundalini Yoga when I was sixteen and a half years old.

February 21, 1989

[When you master] Kundalini Yoga, you will have a perfect, authentic control on your applied intelligence and on all the spheres of life in which you can project, think, bring into thought and understand.

April 18, 1980

I was a Customs Officer at the New Delhi airport and you guys used to come with bundles of money. When you went back you used to go empty, having learned nothing. That's what brought me to the

West and I started teaching Kundalini Yoga, which you cannot even learn in India now. Nobody will teach you, none whatsoever. You are of Judeo-Christian background, so you are untouchables, according to them. I broke every tradition in the world. Then I said, "We'll create yogis, which will come from the West and bless the East."

May 28, 1993

Mahan Tantric

The Mahan Tantric is the healer of the world, filterer of the subconscious for human souls.

November 21, 1991

[A White Tantric Yoga] course is not a teaching with words. It's an experience. So in that experience your physical metabolism and your mental vibration start adjusting and then the results are there. It is a release of energy. We all act like beads. And [like the string of the] prayer beads – there is a one current among us. That is the Divine current. We call it the cosmic current of praana. It is controlled by a Mahan Tantric who is living it, or controls it, and he lifts-up every soul to a potency.

August 3, 1971

Spiritual Teacher

[When you are a teacher,] you serve people and their destinies. You don't serve an individual. The teacher never ever serves an individual. Individuals don't mean anything - just another human body running around. It is the destiny that the body begot that has to be served, to be fulfilled. Otherwise the body will meet its fate.

September 28, 1983

When I came to United States, I told you I have not come here to collect students. I have come here to create teachers. And those created teachers will collect students. Every teacher, every master, has a discipline and it is not for me to love you. It is for me to teach you how to love to live. If you do not know how to love yourself, how you can love me? How can an empty glass give me enough water to quench my thirst?

March 14, 1983

What is a spiritual teacher? A spiritual teacher is nothing but a direct challenge to your life. Direct challenge. You have no concept as Americans of what a spiritual teacher is. You think it to be a swami or a yogi, like, I wear these clothes and I am a spiritual teacher. No, no, no, no. This is absolutely wrong. I am only your spiritual teacher when you say, "I can't do it," and I say, "Shut up and do it."

March 4, 1980

Siri Singh Sahib

I have a title as Siri Singh Sahib that makes me chief religious authority [of Sikh *Dharma*] in the Western Hemisphere. ... There are over a quarter million Sikhs in the Western Hemisphere whom we are supposed to serve. How many we actually serve will depend upon how many call upon us. You have to understand, in the Sikh religion, the higher you are, the humbler you [must be]. That's the policy.

January 16, 1986

Superhealth Drug Rehabilitation Program

Superhealth is our best program. Superhealth is a drug de-addiction program, and in this our proven strength [of success] is eighty to ninety percent people who clean-out from drugs. It's our drug rehabilitation program.

December 2, 1999

Humility

I washed the Golden Temple floor for four and a half years, every day. I was the Customs Officer of all that northern area [of India]. I would come at exactly five o'clock, take off my uniform, wear my simple clothes, and go on the floor and wash the *ParKarma* of the Golden Temple. … I had all the occult powers. … [It took me] four and a half year to get rid of those powers.

7/25/96

[A student] said, "You don't remember, sir. For years I have done my best to slander you left and right, and you never reacted."
I said, "I do remember, and that slander was real."

He said, "May I ask you one question? Why didn't you react?"
I said, "My son, it's a very simple situation. When somebody reacts negatively to me, I just understand at that time how weak I am and how powerful I should be and how better I could serve that person. That's all."

December 10, 1985

To redeem myself, I went to Golden Temple four and a half years and washed the floors of the people who walked there, perhaps for the dust of someone holy enough that my destiny would be changed. That is how I cleansed myself of that ego, and I found my Thou within me.

June 21, 1999

Freedom

You see, I am sixty-seven [years old now, and at] forty-eight I should have gone. I am hanging in there, let's put it that way. But this is called a sense of justice. Everything ever you have given is in the archives. Everything that I earned, and through which I possess, is owned by the *Dharma*.

You see, some of you are stupid. You just fight for a little home, and this and that. I had all the homes and I am myself a tenant. Because what you have, [you will have] to leave later, so leave it now. Do you understand? No, you don't. You don't. You only understand what you understand, "I need a home," "I need this," "I need that." You see, all these ashrams I put it in the **Name** of the One who will always come through. And they are all called Guru Ram Das Ashram. None have my **Name**. I didn't lie to you. I have a Guru and I gave you the Guru and I gave you the Shabad Guru. So you will never be ever be slave to a man. As a free man that I am, I gave you the freedom.

July 26, 1997

How to Use this book

There are many paths to the Infinite and a few of them are shared here. Find ones which speak to you – or select a single one and incorporate that into your life. You have probably heard of actionable intelligence – information that can be acted upon to strategically improve a situation. Well, this is actionable wisdom for you to use and improve yourself. Yogi Bhajan has given us practical wisdom and meditations for us to realize the consciousness of the Divine.

When Yogi Bhajan spoke, it was in the context of a given environment, with students' psyches and emotional/commotional states of being, with certain consciousness, and with world events that were happening. At the same time, he was speaking to the future, children of the children yet to be born – the generations yet to come. He was creating a Divine discourse that carried us to higher realms. He acted as a forklift, and this is how he used to describe himself.

Sometimes, he would say the exact opposite of what he meant, only to create an impact. So decide for yourself what is meant. See which quotes penetrate. Allow your consciousness to compute what resonates.

In this compilation, see what words find a place in your being, uplift you, support you on your journey, and wake you up. If you like, you could read them daily, practicing the wisdom within until you own it for yourself by making it part of your life, part of your being. Some meditations to support this are provided.

You might also make up exercises to incorporate these ways of being, thinking, and experiencing. A simple exercise might be to express gratitude every time you receive a text or every time you see or think of someone you know. If there is a quote you like, repeating it 11-times a day can be helpful to instill it in your consciousness, going deeper and deeper into the experience of it. And as Jugat Guru Singh, Principal of Miri Piri Academy, recently taught in a course on Naad, listen with both ears.

This book can be read from start to finish. Another way is to open it randomly and see what pearls are waiting for you. There is a detailed Table of Contents and index, so you can also look-up a topic. The meditations in the latter part of the book are there to give you a further experience, hopefully to experience Infinity within. If a quote resonates, you might check to see if there is a meditation to take you deeper. Here are some quotes from Yogi Bhajan about the role of meditation and *Japa* (the recitation of mantra) on the path to recognizing your own Infinity:

Meditation

Why do we chant? Why do we meditate? Why do we pray? In our brain, there are neurons, and neurons have patterns. [These patterns develop] our intelligence, our power, our courage, and our strength. So if we do not strengthen the strong patterns of our life to confront our life and to intelligently cope with it, we ultimately do much more wrong to ourselves than we know. When we meditate, pray, and chant, we release the [hidden] subconscious patterns and the real patterns are saved. Life becomes happy, smooth, consistent, cozy, and comfortable.

June 29, 1988

The greatest meditation is when you talk to your own consciousness and your own soul. It is the most fascinating ecstasy of consciousness.

April 11, 1983

Meditation does only one little thing and it's very little in your life. It takes away the power of fear. It takes away fear from your personality.

March 12, 1976

Japa

Defeat can be eaten up by *Japa*, because *Japa* is the repetition of the holy *Nam*, that *Naad* that connects you with God. It's an area code number of the Lord God, the Infinity. It's a *Japa*. *Japa* creates *Tapa*. *Tapa* means the heat that burns up *Karma*. When *Karma* gets burned, then you get to *Dharma*. When you find *Dharma*, it's a path to God.

November 6, 1979

Your effectiveness is what you speak. And your trust is what you speak and deliver. And your respect and goodwill are you delivering again and again and again. That is called *Japa*. *Japa* means jee-paa. Paa means "get", jee means "the soul". Get to the soul. Repeat it, repeat it, repeat it to get to the soul.

July 20, 1988

What God Is

Generate, Organize, Destroy or Deliver

G is to generate the energy.
O is to organize the energy.
And **D** is to destroy the negativity.

October 14, 1971

Your chief executive office is G-O-D:
Generates, organizes and destroys or delivers.

May 7, 1994

God is a three-letter word —
Generate, Organize, and Deliver.
Some people can't even generate.
Some people can generate but can't organize.
Some people can generate and organize
but cannot deliver.
They destroy.
And those who generate, organize, and
deliver are called Khalsa.
They cover the three aspects of God.
They generate the goodwill,
they organize the harmonious existence and
complete merger,
and they deliver the excellence and the
ecstasy of mankind.

October 4, 1992

God Is an Attitude of Gratitude

When you inhale be grateful.
When you exhale be grateful.
Attitude of gratitude is the highest yoga.

January 7, 1974

An attitude of ungratefulness is maya.
An attitude of gratitude is Divinity.
These two decide the whole thing.
You may learn something or not,
but if you have learned an attitude of
gratitude, you are not near God,
you are God.

July 10, 1975

Gratitude is the language of Nanak.
Be grateful.
He created you. He'll take care of you.
He is around you, within you, and He is you!

July 16, 1989

God Is Love

Love is an experience of selflessness within one's self.
And if you have experienced that state of consciousness
then love is God.
Then love is everything.

April 5, 1974

Love is God, my dear.
God is love.

July 9, 1975

One who loves, loves all.
One who loves all, does not love just the one.
When you love all, the One loves you, because you love it.
Learn to love.
And love has no territory.
He who has territory, has not learned love.
Because, how can the Unlimited become limited?
And God and love cannot be separated.
With love, you find God.
How can you be limited and be God?
God is unlimited.

July 9, 1975

The day you understand the meaning of selfless love,
that day God will be in love with you –
God, person, people, environments, unknown faculties,
facilities, wealth, happiness,
all that is contained on this planet.

July 30, 1985

The only God you have is your love.
And God has no dimension.
Ego has every dimension.
So when you are in love, you have no dimension.
When you have dimension, you are not in love.

March 28, 1994

You are hassling and hustling
with the most beautiful gift of life,
the *pranic* energy,
given to you by the creative God
out of pure love.
God is love.
God gives everything out of love.
God even gives to those who hate.
God cannot afford to abandon anybody
because God is everywhere.

June 30, 1985

God Is Profit

If you don't show and convince people that
you can get them a profit,
nobody trusts you or wants you.
The basic motive or moving force is profit. ...
Ultimately, on this planet,
the profit is God.

July 22, 1983

God Is Reality

God Is Reality
A wrench can open the biggest nut of the screw.
But a wrench is only a tool.
I might inspire you to God, but I am only a tool to inspire you.
We are tools.
God and the Word of God are realities.

July 16, 1975

Whenever you cater to your insecurity –
through your frustration,
by your neurosis,
through your imagination, which is totally false –
your false life hurts you and hurts others.
Your real life will never hurt you
and never hurts others,
because reality is God.
It can't hurt anybody.

February 17, 1977

What is God?
The Ultimate Reality,
the Ultimate Truth,
the Ultimate Righteousness.
Not circumstantial,
not environmental,
not individual,
but Infinite Reality.

March, 3, 1980

There is a personal reality,
environmental reality,
and Infinite Reality that is the ultimate truth.

May 6, 1976

Nobility is the representation of God.
Divinity is the strength of God.
Ecstasy is the experience of God.
And the totality is the creation of God.
Reality is God.

July 27, 1983

In the East, God cannot be denied.
It's not an idea.
It's a reality.
In the West, God is an idea –
It can be accepted and can be denied.

Semptember 24, 1983

Moment lived is the moment of God.
Moment denied is the moment of devil.

July 14, 1975

My reality and your reality is God's reality.
Our totality is God's identity.

April 29, 1998

God Is the Creative Psyche

God is the creative psyche through
which you express yourself.

January 24, 1996

A person who can guard his or
her psyche is already guarded by God,
because
the psyche is God, and
God is the psyche.

July 25, 1983

What is God?
A Universal Infinity of the identity of the creature.

June 29, 1976

In this life, it is not your wealth,
not your health,
not your power, and
not your weakness.
It is your commission to identify yourself in the Name of God.

July 8, 1986

The first aspect of Kundalini Yoga is that
the man has a dormant infinity inside.
And the moment man recognizes that infinity
and starts living it,
man is over God.
God is under man.

January 7, 1974

All Creation is that of God.
All relationships are that of God.
All formation is that of God.
All initiation is that of God.
By His Will, the flower blossoms and
by His Will, it withers away.
Who is that mighty gardener who can change
His Will and what can he say?
Because you do not allow the inflow of the
Infinity of God in you,
that's why there is trouble.

July 7, 1994

God is your own Infinite.

July 14, 1975

When we say we belong to God and Guru,
we represent our own Infinity.

July 10, 1975

What is a sin?
God is a sin which makes you realize how
[far] down you have gone.
God is a merit.
He is a virtue that feels you have fulfilled
how high you have come.
Everything is God.
When you do wrong and your
consciousness picks on you,
that is God.

January 27, 1972

What is God?
God is nothing but a human act in
compassion,
kindness, and
truthfulness.

February 22, 1982

[Guru Nanak] was asked, what is God?
And Guru Nanak said,
Jap, Aad Sach, Jugaad Sach, Hai Bhee Sach,
Nanak Hosee Bhee Sach.
In the future, God is Truth,
now God is Truth,
throughout time God was Truth and
in the beginning God was Truth.
Therefore man, you follow the Infinite Truth.
The idea [is] to repeat and speak
Aad Sach, Jugaad Sach, Hai Bhee Sach...
God is Truth.

February 22, 1982

What is God?

Has He six hands, ten heads?

What is He? Is He a matter? Is He a body?

No.

He is a cosmic energy.

It prevails through everybody.

All what we can feel, we can know, or we can imagine is God.

His identity is *Naam* because He is a Truth.

That is why we call Him *Sat Naam*.

He is Yin-Yang.

He is positive-negative.

He is male-female.

He is the Creator and His creation.

September 28, 1969

God Is Truth

Spirit has no relationship to anything except
the purity of Ultimate Truth.
That is what we call God.

April 20, 1975

The truth of creativity, Brahma,
the God consciousness is that which is Infinity.
It is the truth in your action.
It is the righteousness in your action.
It is longing to belong to righteousness.
There is only one path. There is only one path to Godhood.
One path only – that is the path of righteousness
and it requires a sacrifice –
Offering the ego at the altar of the self.
When the ritual is complete out of the totality of nothingness,
then the universal being is born, and you call him a
God-conscious being.

April 13, 1973

Credibility is Divinity.
God's credibility in you is Divinity.

December 11, 1983

God Is Unkown

God Is Unknown.
Unknown of every known is God.

July 20, 1977

Whatever your known is,
that is you.
Whatever your Unknown is,
that is God.

July 10, 1975

Who is God?

What is God?

Can anybody define what God is?

God is nothing but the Unknown of us.

We are nothing but the known of us.

It is the combination of the known and
unknown in harmony,

that will exist in the psyche of the magnetic field,

come through at the frequency of
all vibrations, and

always penetrate and project

the centrifugal and centripetal force
under the circumstances.

And that's called life.

July 25, 1983

When you blend time and space with the Unknown
you become
the beloved of the Unknown.

July 30, 1985

God Is Vibration

God is an energy – vibration.

September 28, 1969

The very concept of God is that God is a vibration.
If you live this concept, you will end up as a God.

October 28, 1969

Try to understand one basic line, one basic word,
God is a vibration.
Concentrate on vibrations.
Try to cause vibrations.
Try to affect other people with vibrations.
Be practical in vibrations.
The moment you start practicing, you will become perfect.
When you are perfect,
you can change the destiny of anybody.

October 28, 1969

Everything is vibration,
and every thought you have is a vibration.
Your body is made up of vibrations. ...
God is the highest vibration.

November 9, 1972

The will of God can be found by tuning one's self
to the sound of Infinity.
This whole universe arises at its vibration and within vibration.
God's breath is the Word,
the *shabad*,
the sound current,
the *Naam*.
And the whole manifestation,
specifically in words,
is the result of that vibration
as it becomes more dense or less dense.

December 3, 1972

Nanak has explained God.
What is God?
Ek Ong Kaar: There is one Creator who has created this creation.
Sat Naam: Truth is His identity.
Kartaa Purakh: The Being who does.
Nirbhau: Fearless. *Nirvair*: Revenge-less.
It is explaining the universe.

July 14, 1975

Akaal Moorat: You are the picture of the deathless God. ...
You must be the picture, the image of the undying God.

June 28, 1987

Ajoonee: Doesn't come in death or birth.
Saibhang: Myself.
Gurprasaad: It is the gift of the Guru.
And where it will come from, there are the orders: *Jaap*.
What's *Jaap*?
Aad Sach, Jugaad Sach, Hai Bhee Sach, Nanak Hosee Bhee Sach.
That's the secret. That's the key.
It's a tragedy in the world.
Somewhere there are locks but no key.
Somewhere there are keys but no locks.

July 14, 1975

Spiritual flow is just like a river.
If anything is taken out of it,
it still continues.

July 6, 1980

God Is You

Penetrate. You are the grace of God.
Project you are the God.
Perceive you are the God.
Project, perceive, penetrate within your own consciousness
because your identity is God.
Prevail, proceed, propel, stop for nothing,
because God in you is alive and well.
This understanding is the joy of all
who trust, believe, and relate to God within themselves.
May you all live in this consciousness.

May 27, 1985

There is a God and the God is you.
And there is no difference between God and you.
And your action decides what God is.
Not anything else.

September 5, 1999

You are nobody and you are everybody.
You are nobody because you are a creature
and you are everybody because you represent the Creator.

September 9, 1978

What is above is below.
What God is – That's what you are.
God is no different than you are.

July 18,1983

God Is Your Positive Self

The problem is – What is God?
In reality, it is your own positive self,
your higher self, your universal self,
self which knows no defeat,
self which can rise
again and again and again
like a wave in the ocean.

July 7, 1984

God is two forces – negative and positive –
energizing within itself.
It's endless.
So it was.
So it is.
Through time it is
and so it shall be.

July 27, 1989

God the Father

Why do we call God the Father?
The father doesn't have a creative nature.
The father can only seed.
We are a soul and a part of that whole Great Soul,
which is the seed in us.
That is why we call God, the Father.
Creativity of sustenance and deliverance comes to the mother,
and that is why we call the Universe, the Mother.

July 10, 1975

Why do they call God as Father?
It's very simple.
God, they call Father because it is
the nucleus, the seed,
and everything else is Creation.

June 20, 1981

Limitations Are Not God

When you are hustling, you are limited.
Once you think you have the Infinite, just think,
look what a bounty
[When] you think you have the Infinite,
you become the Infinite.

January 23, 1974

Take your fear. Take your fear and tell yourself,
"This is my fear," and be afraid to have your own fear.
Out of your life, fear will be gone.
Tell your life, "This is my truth. I am true man. It's my truth."
And then forgive yourself, and forgive your own truth.
You will find the Universal Infinite Truth.
Anything limited that you have found,
if you give it up,
anything infinite will substitute it.

December 31, 1994

What is control?
"Control" is a simple English word that means "to confine."
If you cannot confine something, you cannot control it.
And the moment you confine something, you limit it.
Whatever is limited is not infinite.
Whatever is limited is not God.

June 28, 1983

If you have an ego, you are limited.
If you are egoless, you are unlimited.
With that egoless-ness, God will prevail.

May 17, 1992

Anything which can be defined is not God.

February 23, 1993

There Is No God

[The] question is, why do people pray?
People do not pray to God.
People pray to themselves.
Nobody prays to God. God is a skip-word.
When you are caught, you want trouble.
Now, you should honestly understand.
You will experience what I'm saying to you.
When you are trapped and in difficulty,
you are just becoming a bum.
You can go through a situation —
"Oh my God — my God!"
You know what you are doing?
You are filling your psyche.
You are filling your infinite.
You are expanding from your limits.
God is nothing folks. Don't be fooled.
God is your own residue. Believe me.

July 14, 1975

There is no such thing as God.
… it is just a word which combines three forces:
what creates, what sustains, and what destroys.
And if you want to find God,
the only place you can find God is the English dictionary.
You won't find it anywhere. You have to
write it yourself. [The] choice is yours.
There is no power more than the power of the word,
because God is a word.
Simply, you have to not *talk* the word.
You have to *speak* the word.
That's the secret.

July 2, 1985

You will never say I talk the truth.
You will always say I speak the truth.
You speak the truth. Angels speak.
You talk. And your talking has a hook and bait.
You talk to create, to influence.

July 1, 1985

In our life, I always feel that a day should come
when this realization should come to humanity:
There is no such thing as God and God consciousness.

January 18, 1972

There are no two opinions about it.
There is no God, to be very honest.
It is an imaginative sense of high excellence and infinity.
We created God because God created us.
We wanted to know who created us,
so we Named Him "God."
Some Name Him Allah.
Some Jehovah.
God knows what they do
and what they are going to do tomorrow.

July 20, 1990

If you are not God
then there is no God.

February 18, 1997

Mankind has been taught that God is outside you.
That is the biggest lie.
Your soul is God.
You are just a living God.
Other than you, there is no God.

May 20, 1995

There is no God but your own self.

October 18, 1989

God is neither a secret nor a mystery.
And God doesn't exist.
And there is no such thing as God.
You have been pondering on all these questions uselessly.
Whatever you call God or whatever that mystery is,
and whatever that truth is
for which Guru Nanak sang 1430 pages of *Siri Guru Granth*,
and for which there is the Gita,
and there is the Bible,
and there is the Torah,
and there are the Buddhist scriptures,
– You can read them all.
But, ultimately, I will tell you what God is.
God is a phenomenon practiced by ordinary people
who practice the let-live theory,
who obey the commandment of all commandments:
Thou shalt not kill.
Kill the capacity to kill.
You all talk about peace, but peace will not come.
Kill the war.

February 12, 1985

Why God Is

Will you ever learn
that you are a fountain of light and love
and you have come
from Infinity to finite
to merge in Infinity?
You have to have
your psyche and *pranic* body in balance.

July 18, 2000

Oh, my mind always be with God.
That is why God is unseen.
So you can carry Him around and nobody will bother you.

October 5, 1980

Once a person asked me, "What is liberty? Why is liberation?"
I said, "God created you. You created God.
If you create Earth, you will be Earth bound.
There will be no liberty.
You won't go anywhere because the truth is,
nothing shall go with you."
All that shall go with you is your consciousness.
How many people are consciously conscious
that they have consciousness?

April 2, 1978

Where God is

God Is Found Everywhere

God is not living on the seventh story,
and no lift goes to Him!
God is you.
It is your expression.
It is your identity in existence.
That is why God is everywhere.
Because wherever you are, God is.

January 3, 1972

My dear, finding God is no joke. It is always there.
God is omnipresent and omniscient.
Who is going to find whom?
He is everywhere.
But living God is the life.
Are we willing?
God prevails through His creation.

January 7, 1974

God is everywhere.
So wherever you place Him,
God is there.

June 28, 1983

It is now your time to carry the truth –
to fly the flag and keep it going:
So that you can recognize your own self before yourself;
So that you can exalt yourself before yourself;
So that you can understand yourself before yourself.
God is not anywhere.
God is everywhere.

July 18, 1982

God is everywhere and nowhere.

July 8, 1990

Be conscious that God is God.
Now, the question you can ask is –
Where can I find It?
You can always find God in goodness.
Because if you take away one 'o' from good,
the rest will be God.
So God lives and dwells in goodness.
Ness is the nest of the good and
good is the nest of God.

December 11, 1983

God Is Found in the Dictionary

God is in the English dictionary.
God only exists in the English dictionary.
It is a word. God is a word...
God has been explained in the English dictionary.
Thank you.
It has been explained.
[Yet] still you want to find it.

February 20, 1984

God Is Found in the Word

God is in the word, the word you speak.
That is God – What you say.
And that is God – What you mean to say.
Say what you really mean to say.
Sometimes you say very mean things
and sometimes you say very beautiful things,
but you are very mean inside.
You don't mean what you say.
God is what you say.
In the beginning – What is that?
In the beginning, there was the Word.
Word was with God, and
Word was God.

February 20, 1984

Words are the ultimate power,
and ultimate power is the Word.
Word is God, and God is Word.
There is nothing in between.
The secret and the psychology of the richness
is to speak like God.

July 2, 1985

God Is Found in Truth

When you walk on the path of the spirit,
what is your destination? Home.
And that is God's Home.
Sach khand vasai nirankaar.
Sach khand means the Realm of Truth.

July 22, 1977

Please remember,
if you ever want to go to God,
live a truthful life.
Living in truth is going to God without any hassle.
If you did not live it yesterday,
you could have lived it today.
If you have messed up today, tomorrow be sure [you don't].
Once you start living [a truthful life], you will live forever.
Thus, the mortal can achieve the Immortal.

July 25, 1977

God Is Found in Your Temperament

God is in mental temperament and personal temperament,
out of which kind words are produced.
That is God.
In other words, God is nothing more and
nothing less than kindness in you.
God is not in any religion.
God is not in any ritual.

God is not any people.
God is not any personalities.
God is not in the Word.
God is not outside the Word.
God is not in the center of the Word.
God is not on the top.
God is not at the bottom.
God is not in the hairdo.
God is not in cutting off the nose.
God is not cutting of the neck.
God is not anywhere except in one thing:
When you speak Godly and kind words.
If you want to be elevated, levitated,
and accepted in the court of God,
then speak kind words consciously.

February 20,1984

Lord Krishna died. He was an *avatar*.
What do we remember of him? Gita.
Christ was the Son of God. Not here anymore.
What do we remember of him? Hmm.
In the Bible, Moses was the lawgiver, the messenger of God.
What do we remember of him? What he said in …the Torah.
Guru Arjan Partakh Har personified God.

What do we remember of him? His *shabad* ends
the ***Siri Guru Granth***.
Each word you speak is a combination.
When it affects the other person,
it becomes *Shabad*.
When you speak, it is *Naad*.
When it is gone, then it becomes *Shabad*.
So when you speak,
what you speak,
where you speak,
and why you speak – combined –
is all God in you.
God cannot be outside.
God cannot be inside.
God is that which comes out of your total
personality and mental temperament.
Personal temperament and mental temperament,
when ground together, produce a world.
When mental temperament and personal temperament,
like two wheels, grind together,
a world is produced.

February 20, 1984

God Is Found Within and Without

In reality,
God is equally in balance,
inside and outside.
Microscopically and telescopically,
it is the same God.

July 14, 1982

If you want to see God, you can never find It in yourself.
Because inside is inside.
You want to see God, you have to see It in others.
You cannot see God in yourself.
Can you see your eyes within your eyes?
Find God within others.
That will get rid of your devil.
When you start finding God in others, your devil will run away.

July 19, 1989

Where is God?
God is in each one of you.
And each one of you and your identity
is that God we are talking about.

June 4, 1985

God is part of you and you are part of God,
but you can't feel it as separate.
There is no such thing as God separate from you
or you separate from God!

July 14, 1975

If you realize God is omniscient, omnipresent, and omnipotent,
then you must forget about finding Him.
You have already found Him.
It is in you and you are in Him.

January 3, 1972

God is within you.
Don't talk God – God, God, God.
Where is God?
You are the God.
I can cheat you by saying that I will let you know where God is.
Give me seven hundred dollars and later I will tell you.
You are the God
and that's the answer.
But I am telling you for free.
If it doesn't suit you, pay me.
You are the God
when you act like a God.
And you are also the devil
when you act like a devil.
There is no more God.
There is no less God.

May 7, 1969

God is your own Infinite.

July 14, 1975

Sometimes I wonder why you don't remember that
God is with you.
Have you ever understood and taken mercy on yourself
for all the energy you waste thinking that
you're not wanted, you're not pretty, you're not loved?

July 7, 1986

How many times during the day
do we remember that
God is with us?

July 7, 1986

Where is God?
You are the God.

May 7, 1969

God speaks to us every day here.
There is a consciousness inside.
That is God in us.
Somebody once asked me, "Where is God?"
I said, "Right in you."
In spite of you not liking It, It does talk to you.
You do not listen to It, but It does talk to you.
God is not outside –
God is right inside of every individual, every being.

July 20, 1977

How are you going to find God anywhere?
You are not going to find Him anywhere. Take it from me.
I have gone through every hole and nook and corner.
You will only find God in your own belief.
You are going to find God with your own grace.
You are going to find God with your own wings.
There's no other way.

July 13, 1986

How to Realize God

Self-realization is God realization...
What is your self-realization?
This is yourself.
Know it, feel it, touch it.

June 20, 1972

Thought is power.
God is a thought until not realized.
If you do not realize God,
God is just a thought.

March 27, 1988

By Accepting You Are God

God is in everybody, but what do we do?
You have not come here to find God.
You have come here to remember that you are God.
Just remember,
you are God.

February 10, 1972

You are God.
There is no God beyond you.
First you were born, then you grew up, now you are middle age
or even a little old.
That's your God.
If you see that God in others,
you are Divine.

August 27, 2001

I didn't come here to lay my number on you.
I came here to share with you my happiness, my joy,
my state of bliss.
I vibrated with you.
I don't need to come to teach classes, make money. I had it all.
But I have a responsibility.
Those who seek, I shall answer.
Those who are meek, I shall honor.
Those who want to live, I will grant them happiness.
I am the son of God and you are the children of God.
You are the sons and daughters of God.
You have denied it.
Wake up!
Accept it!
There is no God beyond you.
There was none, there shall be none.
What do you know about when you die?
You die and your senses go, right?
And what is [death] to you?
What will they do to you?
You have no say in it.
It's only when you are born, and you start living,
that you are the living God.
You are.
You are afraid to say it,
because you are afraid to live it,
but it is true.

September 22, 1991

If somehow a woman can remember
that she is
the divine breath of God,
there is nothing that can happen to her.

July 4, 1977

Try to understand that you are
the most vital ultra-power of God.
You only fail when your direction fails.
You are power –
you are energy.
When it is directed towards God,
you are God.
When it is directed towards the other side,
you are the other side.
Everything is you.

July 26, 1983

Bad and good, God, we belong to you and
Ang Sang Whaa-hay Guroo.
That's what we say every day.
Now, they say you must become pure
and then you can relate to God.
It's a lie. It's a lie. It's a lie.
You don't have to become pure.
You have to believe God is with you,
and you will automatically become pure.
It's a catch twenty-two. It is middleman nonsense.
Somebody is cheating you – some rabbi, some yogi, some *singh
sahib.*
Somebody is just playing a game with you.
This is not true.
First, accept God.
Accept it.
You will become good...
Nobody can give you God
and you cannot be good enough to be with God.
You have to do only one good thing –
Accept God is with you.

September 11, 1988

The only thing is,
you religious people have done a dirty job with mankind –
You tell them that there is no God inside
and that they have to see God.
Why does God have to see God, when you are all Gods?
See, within yourself, God.
All problems will be solved.
You shall have no harassment, because God has no harassment.
Infinity has no harassment.
Infinity has no depression.
Infinity has no greed.
Infinity has no attachment.
Infinity has no anger.
If one damn little thing can solve the total problem,
why you are running around like crazy?

May 10, 1996

For two thousand years
you have been told that you have to find God.
You are not going to believe me for one minute.
You are God.
There is no other God.

July 20, 1996

By Acting Like God

Man will start realizing
man is a God,
if he acts like a God.
You will meet people and
they will say, "I am a God,"
and they will act like a God.
They will treat themselves like a God.
They will be full of love and glow.
You will feel in them more calmness than a full ocean,
magnificently projecting love like high tides.
Such children you will experience in a very few, short years.
They will be the same inside.
They will be the same outside.
You will not find them secretive.
They will talk to you about things
that will sound heavy.
It will be solid, it will be truth, it will be like gold.
That is the era in which we are living –
The Aquarian Age –
Age of truth and love – Age of oneness,
when man and God will become one.
Nobody will be the son of God.
Everyone will be the God.

September 16, 1969

Be nothing, or be everything!
Living in between won't work.

July 6, 1980

Those who bow to one master,
the Creator of this universe,
all four corners bow to them.
Those who love manifestation without discrimination,
they become Gods on earth.
Those who give in the Name of God,
their offerings are returned by God, manyfold.
Those who worship,
those who love,
and those who give
are the living God in action.
Those who reach this stage without asking for a return in ego
are perfect Gods in action.
Those who bow in love and seek His protection
shall never experience failure in their life.

April 27, 1969

Life has nothing more to it than this chance –
To become truly divine and truly a channel of God.

July 18, 1983

What is the sign of a God's man? ...
One who, in the beginning of the action,
during the action,
and the end of the action,
remembers
that he or she belongs to the Creator as a creature,
and looks at it without participating in it,
though he is the principal actor in it.

March 23, 1977

Enlightened people do not find God.
They are God.

January 29, 1985

By applying your breath,
you will definitely know,
when unconsciously you breathe eight times [per minute],
you are near God.
When [you breath] four times [per minute],
you are just the perfect image of God.
When one minute means one breath,
you are the living God.
This is the ratio – eight, four, and one.
Normally when you do not do anything,
you breathe about fifteen to sixteen times,
normally sixteen times per minute.
Sometimes you breathe thirty-two times per minute.

May 7, 1969

I believe God gave me this life and
I have to give this life back to God, intact.
And I have to have a code of conduct
that totally tells me I am Divine.

July 25, 1983

Applying Your Breath

The beautiful God has His own beautiful ways.
The tender charge of the Divine comes to us
through the breath.
And if we can consciously breathe
and fill ourselves with the Divine Charge,
we are a living God on earth.
...The greatest thing a man can achieve,
in the shortest time,
is that he can bifurcate the breath.
Take out the tender charge of the Divine,
circulate it in the body to open all the channels,
and be one with Him.
It does not take much time.
What is required is will.
And when we are practicing it,
we will see the results.

April 23, 1969

Life flows through the breath.
So long as you breathe, you are alive.
Your entire life is around your own breath.
We have understood that through the breath,
it is not only the air or the oxygen that you consume,
it is the *pranic* energy, the life force of the entire universe,
that comes to you.
And that life force can be bifurcated
and separated from the breath.
It can be channeled
through the spinal nervous system into the being
so that the cells in the brain can be more open.

July 25, 1971

Do you want to know God in you?
Don't pay a holy man a penny.
Make yourself your own church and altar of God.
God loves you fifteen times per minute,
and that's how you breathe.
Each breath is God's will that you shall live,
and each breath tells you that you shall live.
Therefore, it is so simple –

When you are in any desperation, weakness, or confusion,
just inhale a breath of life
and hold it as a virtue.
Then, let it go when you can't hold it any longer.
If in three breaths you cannot turn your depression into a normal
self,
please call me collect.

August 24, 1991

By Being as You Were Created

You are as God made you.
You are in the image of God.
You are the abstract of God.
This makeup and hanky-panky you do, that is not required.
You are only required to be as God has created you.
This addition and alteration is of your own making.

October 15, 1978

Personal fundamental feeling is
when a person relates to the creative power of God
and you first become as you have been created.
From there, you can walk –
That's the first step.
[The] first honest feeling a person has to realize is to
be as he has to be.
Any addition and alteration in God's kingdom is
either because of the past *Karma*
or the *Karma* you have created.
When you do certain things here on this earth
because you like them,
because it's a passion,
because you are popular,
or because you want to relate to certain things,
then it is your ego working
either out of fear or out of need.

June 14, 1973

You know you want to search for God.
You want to know God.
I think there is something wrong with your brain.
God has already created you!
He knows you.
Just be as you are.
He'll find you.
Why do you want to find Him?
Isn't that very weird?

December 6, 1973

By Being Friends with the Unknown

Instead of being afraid of the unknown,
make the Unknown your friend.

May 17, 1983

I know the Unknown is known to me.
This is the capacity of every woman –
to manifest God.
This is the secret of manifesting God.
And what is the Unknown?
Unknown is the totality.
Known is the confinement.
Known has to know the Unknown,
has to experience the Unknown,
has to deal with the Unknown,
has to find the Unknown,
has to walk into the Unknown.
Unknown is unknown.
But when you take a pattern of friendship,
"I know the Unknown is known to me,"
then it gives you inner confidence that is called
equilibrium and total stability.

August 14, 1978

By Being Silent

God has a language called silence.

September 11, 1994

In absolute silence, you can hear the voice of God within you.
Bring your body into absolute silence, thoughtlessness, and
absolute stillness.
Silence moves the universe.
Breathe deep.
Breathe consciously and mechanically, long and deep.
In stillness, there is oneness.
In oneness, there is God.

May 15, 1998

Language of God is mental silence.

December 10, 1972

Silence is the language of God.

June 18, 1981

By Channeling Your Desire Towards God

If you have terrible anger and you use that
anger on your negative side,
you will become positive in no time.
If you are very, very lustful and you lust for Almighty God,
you will become the highest saint on the planet.
If you're really attached and you get
attached to your consciousness,
people will bow to you.
And if you are very greedy, honestly selfish and greedy,
just understand that the Giver of everything is God.
You will have richness that nobody can touch.
These five enemies of yours are smart, and
they are out to get you.
But you can use them. …
I take pride in being unattached in the most attached situations.
I take pride in looking at things from another point of view.

July 21, 1983

Life creates desire.
To become desireless is a desire –
a very high, powerful desire.
As long as there is life, there will be desire.
As long as there is desire, there will be life.
They both end at the same time.
Channel the desire.
Desire God.

July 18, 1983

I don't want you to not have desires.
If you don't desire God,
how are you going to get It?
But don't run after God.
Desire that your activity be dedicated to God.
Don't try to find out what you already have found out.

September 28, 1985

By Dedicating Yourself to God

The only concept of this human life is *Nith* and *Nimith*.
Nimith is for the sake of –
If you live for the sake of God,
you become God.
And *Nith* means that you live for your own sake.
Then you live to come and go
and it is called *Avagavan*, coming and going.

June 24, 1979

If you say you are alive because of God,
you say you are giving things because of God,
you say you are taking things because of God,
you dedicate things to God,
that is called *Nimith*,
all for the sake of God.
Nith means that your everyday affairs
shall be taken care of.

February 7, 1988

It is time to dedicate yourself to God.
It is time to relate very deeply
to the Word of the Guru and to the blessing of God.

July 17, 1983

If you live for the sake of God,
whatever you have [belongs to] God,
or it carries the Name of God –
you owe no *Karma*.
But if it carries your Name,
it carries your *Karma* with it.

February 7, 1988

These are two secret fundamental criteria of a divine woman –
She always feels the presence of God, and
She always dedicates every action to God.

July 4, 1977

Never feel handicapped.
The power of the *Shabad* is,
"In the beginning was the Word,
and the Word was with God, and the Word was God."[1]
You have the Word of God,
sung by those who have realized God.
That's the power of the *Shabad*.
So, what I am saying to you is never, ever feel handicapped.
Nobody can make you handicapped.
And if feelings are so heavy that
you do not know what to do,
bow before the Guru, and put them before the Guru.
Let Guru take care of it.
The art of dedication is an art of realization
and is a loyal art of self-experience
through which God is experienced and Guru is instilled.

February 8, 1987

If you dedicate yourself to God, you shall reap God.
If you dedicate yourself to earth, you shall reap the earth.
It's a very simple thing.

April 12, 1982

1 John 1:1, New International Version Bible

By Doing Service

… There is something called *Seva*
which is done with your heart and head both.
It is done in the Name of God,
in obedience to God,
and for the sake of God.
What that brings, no man can give you.

July 28, 1982

Seva is a conscious and deliberate service
to benefit another person,
even at your cost.
And remember,
whosoever does *Seva*
is the one in a hundred that God comes through.

September 9, 1990

Serve God,
love God,
and be God.
Or serve ego,
love ego
and be ego.

February 1, 1985

What is Divinity?
When you serve all without duality
and tolerate [all]
because God's spirit [is] in you.

October 11, 1987

With this body, serve God in everybody.
Don't serve a person –
Serve God in a person.
That's the only way to be divine.

May 31, 1992

Seva or service is infinite giving.
Service is not finite giving.
If you do some service and say, "I served,"
then you have totally missed the point.
Service is when you feel honored by doing something.
You don't feel honor in the company of many,
you feel it within your own self.
That is service.
Seva is when you are honored on the inside,
when you honor yourself.
When I am honored in my consciousness
for doing something,
it is *seva*.

July 22, 1978

If you start serving others
and seeing God in them,
you have reached the status of
God within you.

May 7, 1994

If you make life a *seva*,
your pain will go away.

August 1, 1982

Those who serve without expecting anything,
God and mother nature serve them.

January 24, 1996

When God is around you,
in you,
and with you,
then God worships you
because you serve God.
That is what *seva* is.

July 18, 1982

Service, *seva*, gives you territory.
Serve somebody and
he'll be grateful to you for the rest of his life.

July 1, 1991

By Doing These Three Things

If you can do these three things, you'll find God:
Number one, don't let yourself down,
don't let anybody else down,
and do not participate in organizing
a letdown of another person.

September 29, 1993

By Dwelling in God – Trusting in God

We don't say, "In God we trust."
We say, "In God we dwell."

June 23, 1997

Those who dwell on Him,
God dwells in them.

May 27, 1979

Fearless.
Nirbhau, Nirvair.
Nirbhau, you become fearless
when the love of God comes so near you
that you not only trust in God,
you dwell in God.
You are afraid of no one.

April 5, 1981

You came from God and
you will go to God.
All things come from God and all things go to God.
That is a fact.
If all things come from God
and all things go to God,
then where do you stand?
Then, your permanent home is God.

July 5, 1981

Without trust, you cannot be happy.
There is nothing else to trust except God because God is Infinite.
Everything is finite.
The finite must be destroyed.
What is the secret of happiness?
Trust in God.

July 25, 1977

Trust in God and
dwell in the Almighty.

June 28, 1999

When you dwell in God, you are in It.
You are in love with It.
You are enjoying It.
It is all perfect.
Remember,
love without trust and trust without love mean nothing.
Love is nothing but infinite trust.
Infinite trust is nothing but love.

April 5, 1981

By Dwelling in Reverence

Infinity cannot be measured.
Reverence cannot be explained,
because reverence is Infinity.
Reverence has such a power that it becomes Infinity,
and for you to become Infinity,
you have to have self-reverence,
not reference.

July 26, 1996

When you are afraid to lose your own reverence
then you become divine,
then you become modest,
then you learn everything,
then you have discipline,
then you have success.

September 6, 1990

Where there is reverence,
where dwells the reverence,
God dwells.

September 6, 1990

It's a very old couplet where there is a reference to reverence,
even God dwells there.
And the person who practices becomes
always immortal and infinite.
Reverence of self and to all the selves
that the self sees,
creates the bondage of infinity
in an active experience of the light of God.
Bondage is there, and you are bound by Infinity.
Prosperity, reality, all comes to you.
Every opportunity, every gift of life, will be around you.

September 6, 1990

By Experiencing Cosmic Consciousness

[The] moment you start acting constantly with consciousness,
you start becoming God.
That is the first step to becoming God, healthy God.
And then you have to smile,
you have to talk,
you have to have patience,
you have to help people,
you have to be good.
That is the happy God.
Be the greatest giver,
don't tease anybody,
don't upset anybody,
don't talk ill of anybody,
don't see ill in anybody,
then you will be the holy God.
This way you have to manufacture in you
healthy, happy, and holy God.
That is the God in you.

April 23, 1969

Be liberated when you are alive.
After death, my friend – those who do not have the keys now,
do you think they are going to open the door
when they reach home?
Are you kidding?
Who are you making a fool of?
After death, Christ will come and talk to you?
Are you crazy?
When you are alive, if he has not talked to you,
after death why should he bother?
Talk when you are alive.
After death, you cannot think about it.
Life has been given to you to experience.
Experience it if you want to experience
Christ consciousness now.
Experience God consciousness now.
Experience the Buddha consciousness now.
Or seek like *Nanak*,
so that you can produce another *Angad*.

July 14, 1975

My friend, learn to never wake up without meditation
nor without thanking your own Unknown – your God.
And never sleep without meditation
nor without relating to your own Unknown – God.
Who knows if tomorrow shall dawn on your home?
Keep the account clear.
See the day with God.
Start the day with God,
then God will take care of it.
Isn't it simple?
Rise and see the seeker of God.
And at the end of the day,
give yourself to God and sleep.
If the morning dawns on you again, get up.
From moment to moment, day to day,
walk away with the precious gift of life.

July 14, 1975

God has to be reached by these three stages:
first is the individual consciousness,
second is the group consciousness, and
third is God consciousness or the cosmic consciousness.

November 11, 1970

By Experiencing Innocence

The law of polarity, of negative and positive, is a circular law. ...
So, there is good and evil.
If you do not know the depth,
if you do not know the height,
that is a very unfortunate thing in spiritual people.
They want to study the height of God,
but they don't want to study what God is not.
So, if you do not study what ... God is not,
you can never know what God is.
You have to know evil to know good.
So, what is bad and good? You have to know both.
You want my point of view?
Try to know nothing.
Your innocence will make God serve you.

January 1, 1969

Innocence is God.
God is innocent.
Sat Naam is *Satya*, the purity.
When you are innocent,
you cannot be provoked,
you cannot be perverted,
you cannot be polluted,
you will be safe and always loved.
Believe me.

May 31, 1983

Do you know what God is?
God is the innocence within you.
God is not your crookedness,
your fears,
your degrees,
your power, or
your politics.

August 16, 1992

By Experiencing Your Divine Nature

You have come in this world to know about nature,
to learn about nature.
God can be realized through the nature around you.
God can be realized through your very own nature.
Your very nature will represent you
whether you are divine or you are evil.
If man, by nature, is very delicate and compassionate,
he is divine.
If by nature he is ugly, selfish, and without compassion,
he is a demon.
And how is this nature built?
It is built in three years in the school of the mother.
[The] first three years of a person's life
are the greatest schooling on this planet.
Whatever impact a child gets in those three years,
that lays the basic fundamentals of the child
for the entire period to come.

January 18, 1972

By Forgiving

Forgiveness is the highest act.
But if you are a teacher,
and you forgive and you forget,
then that is not spiritual integrity. That is a copout.
Just understand – the thing that is good for one,
is the worst for another.
Don't misunderstand that something is good for all.
If a spiritual teacher forgives or forgets, he is a copout.
He commits a sin.
But for an ordinary person, to forgive and forget is a divine act.
What is divine for an ordinary person is
undivine for a spiritual man.

April 10, 1984

When a person forgives beyond any concept,
concession, jurisdiction, territory, or condition,
then the person becomes infinite,
and that is Divinity.

December 27, 1994

All this pain is logical, psychological, and factual
and it is because you are not forgiving God for
separating you from Him.
So, first, please forgive God that
He separated you from Himself
and created you as a creature. …
Secondly, forgive your destiny that it is as it is.
You never wrote it. You earned it, and you forgot about it.
But that's the way it is and that's the way it is. …
Thirdly, forgive the distance and the environment,
which are always challenging, the cause and the affect. …
And the fourth forgiveness is, forgive your capacity, your ability,
your duality, and your Divinity. Please forgive it.
It is limited.
The job of the Infinite is the infinite job –
just keep doing it and feel comfortable
He knows it better because God is everywhere,
and we are just somewhere.
Finally, forgive yourself that you have to go through it.
That is the most important.
We are very cruel to ourselves.
We are very cruel to our being.
We are very cruel to our grace.
We are very cruel to our own tolerance.

December 31, 1991

Some actions of yours make you give.
Then, you are divine.
And some actions of yours make you forgive.
Then, you are God.

September 24, 1998

By Four Ways

Beauty of a woman is that
without woman, there is no God.
She is the most powerful human creature.
Man has only one way to be liberated –
that is to be a man of God.
Woman has four ways, so she is a superior being.
She can give birth to a man of God.
She can serve a man of God.
She can be a man of God.
And she can create environments
to make somebody to be a man of God,
which man can't do.

June 29, 1976

By Giving Yourself to God

A sinner can become a saint right now
if they decide that yesterday is gone,
today is me, and
tomorrow will be God.
That is how you give yourself to God.

July 3, 1984

Give yourself to God and Guru,
mind and soul.

August 3, 1977

If you give yourself unto Infinity,
it will give back to you tenfold.

January 22, 1979

Give yourself to God
and enjoy it.
It's a state of enjoyment,
which is more than anything you understand.

November 24, 1981

When you have totally given yourself to God consciousness
and you live in the state of bliss while alive,
then there is no pain that can upset you.

October 28, 1972

You have to give yourself your God
and that is within you.
Feel divine.
Quote. "Feel divine, duality will go away.
The moment duality goes away,
all happiness will come to you."
This is a simple formula.

April 15, 1997

By Having Endurance unto Infinity

It is called endurance because the mind is
not subject to time and space.
When a person's mind can endure beyond time and space,
it can be the manifested God. …
When you manifest a powerful limit to yourself,
you feel you have reached an end.
That is where endurance starts.
If you can dare to have the courage to go beyond that end,
that's what endurance will be.

July 3, 1990

Your character should extend into Infinity.
[Infinity] should be your nomenclature.
Your endurance should take it right to the end of Infinity. …
Love is Infinity, and Infinity in action is called endurance.

December 24, 1987

By Listening to the Guru's Words

Basically, *Gurbani* means the Guru's words,
what the Guru spoke.
That is the imprint of the essence.
That is the pathway.
So, what the Guru spoke,
if an ordinary human being shall speak that,
it will always elevate you to that state of consciousness.

February 28, 1977

The whole of *Gurbani* has one meaning –
It makes a person divine. ...
The sound current of the *Shabad* is such a combination,
that it makes you divine.

July 5, 1978

There is nothing good and
there is nothing bad in this world,
thinking makes it so.
Let your thinking enrich you.
Let your thought enrich you.
Let your thought produce God.
How that will happen?
Where can you go?
Where can you get that power?
That's why I say, go to the *Siri Guru Granth.*
That's your Guru.
It will talk to you,
it will speak to you,
it will explain to you, and
it will give you that joy which is forever yours.

January 29, 1985

Word is very important.

Word is very fundamental.

It's very realistic.

It's God.

And how can God be reached?

It can be reach through the Word.

From what word?

From Guru's word.

Guru's words are very important.

Human words are not important,

because humans are not enlightened.

They can change.

They can be emotional.

They can be negative.

They can be positive.

They can be circumstantial.

They can be purposeful.

They might be using words as bait.

February 15, 1987

If your anchor is God and Guru's word,
Guru's words are your anchor.
It keeps God in your heart –
seated, planted, and residing and presiding
and it goes on.
That's the truth.

Arpil 29, 1985

The sole purpose of human life is
to befriend your own soul.
And that is why Guru's words are there –
to make you understand,
bring you to understand,
so you can understand
and stand under
in this most beautiful, most cozy, most far-out environment
where you can excel,
resurrect, and
be one with God.

July 10, 1988

By Living in the Now

The moment you live in the moment,
God is with you.
And the moments you waste thinking about it,
you have given it to the devil.
Each moment of life is given to you
as a gift by the Giver.

July 14, 1975

I don't believe in time and space.
I believe in now.
Get to God now.
Experience God now.

January 29, 1985

By Living Life in Reality, Not in Denial

Life is a reality, a very powerful reality.
And you don't understand it at all.
Life has nothing more to it.
This is the only chance when you can really become
truly divine and truly a channel of God,
and you can truly represent God.

July 18, 1983

God doesn't get angry with anybody.
God doesn't take revenge on anybody.
God doesn't deny anybody.
One who denies another person, has nothing to do with God.
Denial is not God.
But where is the courage in us to accept that whole thing?
Here, at the third center, we can be totally unique, perfect.
Our presence can work.
We can be beautiful without any setup and charm,
if we have our third center working for us.

February 5, 1991

By Meditating and Merging

Meditation is when you put yourself above the self,
when you open yourself.
The moment you open yourself above the self,
you enter into a state of higher consciousness or a higher self.
And the moment you enter into a state of higher self
you become merged with the Universal Consciousness.
Those few moments of Universal Consciousness
are much better and much brighter than all the moments you
have lived through.
And when the Universal Psyche merges with your individual
psyche,
it gives you strength,
it gives you power, and
it makes you a very strong magnetic personality.
And thus, you have the path of life sorted out.

September 26, 1972

By Not Reacting

Do you know when you don't react,
you are immediately identified as a God?
Do you know?
How does this known become unknown immediately
when you do not react?
Do you know?
Hey, am I telling a lie or the truth? How many of you know?
This known becomes unknown the moment you do not react.
When you react, you are known.
When you don't react, you are unknown.
Why you are trying to find the Unknown?
All you have to do is not react.
You are running after everything and doing all those things.
This is one simple thing that you have to practice –
Do not react.
When you do not react, you are unknown.
So why try to find the Unknown
when you are already unknown?

October 12, 1972

God realization is when you have so much self-control
that opposite pairs do not disturb you.
That is God realization –
When fame and shame do not bother you.
When you are so mentally saturated
and feel one with Him
that opposite pairs do not affect you.
It is not that you can control it or not.
It does not affect you at all.

April 22, 1969

Now, it is my understanding that you react under fear.
My feeling is that when a person has trust in God,
then there is no fear –
And when there is no fear, there is no reaction.
Under these circumstances,
you let the Divine create the sequence
and the consequence
and you enjoy it.
Rather than living the harshness of life,
you watch the drama of life.

April 5, 1981

The neutral mind is the power of balance
in which a person can become God,
experience being God,
and still enjoy all the faculties of being human.
Then, nothing can stop you.
Even the angels are jealous of humans because of that.

June 15, 1995

Look to tomorrow.
Today is already going away.
Why run after it? Don't run after time. Run after nothing.
Be there and let tomorrow come.
Patience pays.
Stand still and wait.
Tomorrow will bring all that today couldn't,
good and bad both.
If you are radiant,
you will see everything in the light.
If you are dark,
in the darkness you will see nothing although things are there.

June 28, 1983

The first job of life is to
confront negativity
and penetrate through it.

June 29, 1983

First comes emotion.
The next stage after emotion is anger.
The stage after anger is frustration,
and the stage after frustration is neurosis.
These are the stages you have to go through.
The first stage is to be unemotional.
The next stage is to become conscious,
and the third stage is to become clear.
The fourth stage is to become illumined, to become enlightened.
The base is the same.
Whoever can control his emotions
can guide his own destiny.

July 18, 1983

By Power of the Word

"In the beginning was the Word,
and the word was with God
and the word was God"[2].
[The] power of the Word is infinite.
That is why the words we speak
is what we are known for,
and that is what we are.

April 18, 1974

When you tell a man, "You are a donkey,"
actually, he is not a donkey, he is a man,
but you transmigrate him with the power of the word.
And when you tell a man, "You are an angel,"
you incarnate him because you are in the true image of God.
You have the power over matter, and your energy is your word.
It really does impact some people.
Some people really feel that they are donkeys,
and some really believe, at that moment, that they are angels.

April 18, 1974

2 John 1:1, New International Version Bible

The power of the word of God
is such that whosoever speaks
through the tongue
will purify the entire being
and a purified being becomes God, always and forever.

July 18, 1983

By Projecting the Realization that God Is Within

God is realization within the self.
Projecting that realization
into practical action
makes a person God.

May 7, 1969

Jesus came and he said, (according to the Gospel of Thomas)
"In heaven, there is the kingdom of the Father
and it can be within you if you realize it."

May 23, 1973

When a person realizes their total unknown potential
within their own self
and they become consciously conscious
and they experience their total unknown potential
within themselves,
that person becomes totally enlightened
about their total being.

May 23, 1973

By Putting the One Before Everything

That is what *Guru Gobind Singh* did for you –
He gave you the *Siri Guru Granth,* the *Shabad Guru.*
If you put *Shabad Guru* before you,
then you become *Gurmukh.*
Then, your wisdom will come through and
it will please everybody, and
then everybody will love you and serve you.

April 24, 1988

The purpose of life is that mission of
finding Infinity in your strength,
that one Infinity, that one *Ek Ong Kaar*, in your own practical life.
And how do you to do that? It's very simple.
Put One before you.
You are *Ong Kaar* – you are a creative orbit-consciousness of
God.
Ong Kaar means God in creation.
You put One, [Ek], before it.
Why? Because your Guru, Guru Nanak, said it that way.
So, you always learn from the teacher.
Put One before you.

April 24, 1988

Put One before everything.
Prefer One before everything.
Give priority to the One before everything.
Every action of your life must have the One before it, not after it.
Guru Nanak didn't say, "Ong Kaar Ek." Did he? Did he?
He said, "*Ek Ong Kaar*."

April 24, 1988

Put One before everything.
And that One is Infinite –
Your own Creator –
Your own consciousness.

April 30, 1988

Put One before everything.
And what is that One?
All is One.

May 15, 1988

By Talking About God

Nanak said, "Whenever you sit,
talk about God and men of God."
What will that give you?
That will give your you to you.

July 14, 1975

Somebody asked me once,
"What is the quickest way to become a holy man?"
I said, "Close all your holes and use your central hole,
your mouth, to talk about God."
He said to me,
"Now, I am telling you a living story.
It is not something from the last incarnation."
And I said to him,
"Whatever you sow,
whatever you do,
just say, *Sat Naam*."
He said, "Nothing else?"
I said, "Nothing else."
Four years have gone by,
and he has become totally *Sat Naam*.
In your life, whatever the moment brings you,
it will come moment to moment.
If in that moment you talk about God,
live about God,
work about God,
you become God.

July 14, 1975

By Tuning the Mind into the Soul

I was asking for an answer –
How could *Guru Arjan* sit on that hot plate,
and why couldn't we all sit?
That was the basic thing.
And basically, when God is with everyone
and all are in the image of God,
why are some like that?
Why are some not like that?
I had already been trying to do, what he went through.
Then finally the answer came.
There are some who, from the base of God,
get to the Guru as a guide,
and they trained their mind to have power over their soul.
Their mind does not work on matter.
Their mind does not work on mind.
Their mind works on soul.
And these are the few blessed ones who tune-in,
into that little hook, which is known as
individual identity of the supreme consciousness.
In the mystic world, we call it soul.
Once that contact is established,
then the universal soul is realized,
and the power of the universal soul is realized.

June 3, 1973

By Vibrating and Moving in Rhythm

God is everything, everywhere.

It is a dance of trinity. ...

Electron, proton, and neutron –

First right eye, left eye, and third eye –

This dance is the universe.

This universe is God.

This God is the dance.

Vibration is God.

God is vibration.

And when you meditate on a certain sound current,
known as *Shabad*,

those vibrations and that rhythm bring

the totality of the rhythm into the rhythm.

You vibrate on Infinity.

Infinity vibrates on you.

When this rhythm is created, man is in ecstasy.

He is God.

November 9, 1971

When the vibrating nucleus
realizes the magnetic field of its own psyche
in relationship to the magnetic beat of the universal psyche
and thus creates a harmony,
then the merger is Infinity.

October 2, 1972

This being has a trinity,
which constitutes the self.
And this trinity vibrates at the rate
that depends upon its connection with the Supreme supply line.
We presume to call it God. …
Trinity – electron, proton, and neutron – they dance.
Their existence is their dance.
In Hindu mythology, they call it the dance of Shiva.
They believe three gods dance:
Brahma – the god of creation,
Vishnu – the god who sustains, and
Shiva – the god of death.

June 18, 1972

The moment you cross three-point-five frequency of your psyche,
God starts becoming a teeny-tiny thing and
you start becoming Almighty.
There is a complete shift. ...
God can come to a human experience
when people get to a frequency where they can
go beyond three-point-five electromagnetic psyche.
And the highest achievement of that point is
between one-point-five and two-point-five.

March 6, 1991

If you create that rhythm –
the best rhythm is that
the harmony of the universe should serve you
in the harmony of the essence,
and the self of the molecule in the self
of the beat of the heart
and the self of the rhythm of the universe
you want to conquer.
Therefore, you must follow the beat of the heart
or the beat of the breath.
Both beats are going to create a rhythm
between the ecology of the universe
and physiology of your existence.

October 3, 1996

By *Walking the Path of* Dharma

Now, I'll tell you something which nobody else will tell you.
When you decide that you are going to walk
on the path of *Dharma*,
God will come to you –
You need not go to God.
But the secret is to keep going.
Because while you are going,
you can never reach God.
He is everywhere and He is nowhere.
But one thing will happen –
Once you become mentally determined that
"I am the *Dharma* and *Dharma* is me,"
then God is not far away.

July 22, 1977

By Your Body and Senses

Your body is your best friend.
Without it, you cannot exist.
And God realization cannot be achieved,
even by God,
without coming into the body.

April 20, 1969

If you master your body, this body,
these nine gates of the body –
If you can master them,
all secrets of nature and God will open to you.

September 28, 1969

There are nine gates in the body:
two ears, two eyes, two nostrils, one mouth,
two downstairs – you all know this.
So, that makes nine.
If these nine gates are watched and
the things that go in and come out are righteous,
you are holy.
And if these holes are allowed to be misused,
you will suffer from that part of holey-ness.

December 4, 1973

The question is very simple and I'll put it in a simple way,
"Are we born to suffer?"
It's a simple question and the answer is simply,
"No."
Then the question arises,
"Why do we suffer?"
Again, the answer is simple –
It is because we forget the pivotal power,
the central power,
the fulcrum power of our divinity and our divine concept,
which is God – G-O-D.

God is the generating power,

the organizing power, and

the destroying power.

So, if we don't organize what we generate or create,
it will destroy us.

If there is heat, the wind will rise, the cold air will blow,
and the rain will follow.

It is called the law of the cycle.

When we do not organize, we create destruction.

On this planet, everything that God has created is organized.

The sun, the mighty sun that guarantees life,
rises on time and sets on time.

The moon waxes and wanes on time.

You will not find anything, creative and constructive,
that is not on time.

I can tell you what is off-time: earthquakes,
volcanic eruptions, unpredicted storms.

These are all destructive forces.

Snow storms and avalanches are offbeat,
off-time, off-balance – messengers of destruction.

What do humans have?
Anger, attachment, sensuality, greed.

In our caliber, they are nothing but
unpredictable phenomena.

July 30, 1980

We have to be more careful about losing something
than about getting something.
We have to get slowly and must not forget Hazrat Musa's story.
...
He used to go and call to God every day.
And the voice used to come from beyond the hill –
This is this, that is that, and then he would tell the people.
One day he insisted, "I want to see you."
The voice said, "Musa, the awareness in you is right,
but the body you have is not so channeled
to take this that I am."
He said, "Whatever you are, come out."
Thrice, he was told not to insist.
And when that awareness came,
that light of the billion suns,
Musa lost his eyesight.
If Hazrat Musa cannot stand that awareness,
who are we?
Therefore, I just want to tell you,
build up yourself and your channels,
deservingly beautiful,
to receive that Divine Charge in you as fast as possible,
and it will come to you.
Have faith.
Faith moves the mountain;
otherwise, stones are heavy for a person.

April 20, 1969

You see, you can't have
God awareness
or self-realization
or consciousness
until and unless you are fit enough
to hold in you the Divine Charge.

April 25, 1969

The purpose of life on this Earth is
to realize God through the senses.
That's why the soul is given five *tattvas to reside in*:
ether, air, fire, water, and earth.
These five *tattvas* make up your physical body.
And this body lives because there is a soul in it.
And when the soul is in these five *tattvas,*
there are five main senses.
The combination of senses make you feel yourself.
In exactly the same way you realize yourself
is the same way to realize God.
So, what it boils down to is that
you have to realize God through the senses.

If you reach that common sense, or the sixth sense,
or the creative sense, or the sexual and
sensually created sexual sense –
Call it anyway you want, call it G energy, Chi energy,
this energy, that energy, consciousness, super consciousness.
Call it love. Call it anything.
The fact is, in this human body, you have to realize God
sensibly through the senses.
And, in other words, it is as simple as this:
You act and live,
act and live.
But your actions and your living
should be Godly, should be Divine.

November 11, 1984

Through Bana, Bani, Seva, and Simran

Four things: *Seva, Simran, Bana, Bani.*
Bana is given to you
so that the presence of God can work through you.
Your whole motivation should be to prepare for God.

August 1, 1982

Through your presence,
everyone should feel that you are divine – *Bana*.
Then Bani – Through your word
everyone should feel that you are divine.
Through Seva – Through your deeds,
everybody should be elevated as divine.
Simran – Through that powerful *Sadhana*,
you should be elevating yourself.
There are four ways to go.

August 1, 1982

Through *Simran*, you can charge yourself.
Through *Seva*, you can elevate any worry.
With *Bana*, God's presence can work through you.
Through *Bani*, God can be communicated through you.
In your presence, through your presence, by your presence,
God can serve other people.
And through *Bani*, God can be communicated to other people.
Through *Seva*, you can elevate other people.
Through *Simran*, you can always elevate yourself.
So, the process is very complete.

August 1, 1982

Four things: *Seva, Simran, Bana, Bani.*
Bana is given to you
so that the presence of God can work through you.
Your whole motivation should be to prepare for God.

August 1, 1982

Through Your Caliber and Capacity

Let us do a very earnest job because,
in my faith,
I believe that God acts through all human beings equally.
You simply have to switch your caliber
from your individual insecure self
to your infinite and higher self.

July 18, 1983

God gave you a thing called caliber.
God gave you caliber, so you should have capacity.
You should have capacity to develop endurance,
which will be perpetual.
Then, nobody can defeat you.
Then, you shall never lose.

August 18, 1990

Emotional caliber limits you – It is finite.
Devotional caliber makes you infinite – It is one-pointed.
Nothing can stop it.
There's no question, no answer.
"Theirs not to reason why,
Theirs but to do and die.
Into the valley of Death
Rode the six hundred."[3]
We remember them. ...
The "Charge of the Light Brigade"
is remembered as the most heroic act.
Because as gold is tested in the fire,
man is tested in adversity.

June 12, 1978

---

3   Alfred, Lord Tennyson – *Charge of the Light Brigade*, 1854

Through Communication

You can achieve everything through communication.
You are what you say.
Whatever you say, you become.
Those who meditate on God
become God.
Those who talk about God
become God.
Those who propagate or serve God
become God.

December 17, 1983

Everything has a key.
This is the key to find God all the time:
Start speaking the language of God
and, in a shortest possible time,
you will be God.
Live as God lives,
talk as God talks,
communicate as God communicates.

January 24, 1973

There's a frequency of a human being,
and communication is the biggest essence of a divine man and Godly man.
What is it?
He's noble.

May 9, 1978

Communication is the essence of life.
It is life, indeed.
Those who communicate like God
are those in whose heart God lives.

May 9, 1978

The Laws of Infinity to Realize God

God is the Doer

One thing to remember is –
All things come from God and all things go to God.

July 26, 1977

One thing to remember is, all things come from God and all
things go to God...
If you ever want to recreate your equilibrium
when you are out of balance,
just repeat it loud and clear.
Verbalize it.

July 19,1977

The One who sent me here
will take care of me.

August 17, 1978

If the Creator can take care of this whole incarnation,
if God can rotate this planet earth,
can't He take care of your routine?

July 19, 1979

Do you know what is wrong with you?
I will tell you the fundamental wrong which I feel –
You feel YOU can make it,
and I feel God makes it.
That is the total game here.
I feel I should be very simple and keep going and
if God wants something for me,
He's going to do it.

July 25, 1983

There are two ways to live –
Either you work or God works for you.

July 1, 1983

When you act, God is silent.
When you are silent, only then, God acts.

June 30, 1994

When you accept God and
do not accept that God is the doer,
then you have NOT accepted God.

April 3, 1994

Whatever the result will be,
that shall be God's grace.

June 29, 1986

The Will of God is nothing but
accepting the role of Infinity.

September 3, 1978

Five Cosmic Laws – How to Be God

The one who knows these five secret laws can be the most
creative happy person.

◆ First cosmic law is that you depend on the Cosmic Energy
as a beloved depends on the fragrance of the lover. In every
moment of distress, you do not look to any other power
except the one Creator, the Cosmos. You shall never, never be
unhappy.

◆ Second law is that when you realize truth, you will speak
truth, you will practice truth, and you will not let anything
enter your aura which is not truth. You will be the living God!
The question of unhappiness cannot arise.

◆ Third cosmic law is that if you do not dwell on or create any
action with a negative force that can build up a negative cage
around you, you will always live happy.

◆ Fourth cosmic law is that when you are the giver, you will
never be the beggar.

◆ And the fifth cosmic law is that you will always be the custodian
of the Creator Divine, and the breath is the gift to you.

If you remember these five cosmic laws,
there is no power which can destroy you.
Even God shall ask before dealing with you…
I have given you five cosmic laws –
How to be God.

May 9, 1969

Laws of God

Those who love life will never take a life.
Those who love the grace of God
will never disgrace anybody.
It's a simple law.

February 20, 1984

The law is simple.
When I withdraw and draw the entire universal mind within me,
I am the master of the universe.
But when I go out of my shell,
then I am a little tiny creature who is seeking
what has not been found.
Within me, I can find the greatest find of all finds.
That is me,
within me.

March 22, 1975

The law of language
is that within eight sentences,
you must dedicate your conversation to God.
This is a law.
If you read *Gurbani*, **Siri Guru Granth**,
within eight sutras is the entire conversation,
the entire message,
the whole thing.

July 3, 1977

Those who love God live for others.
Those who hate God live for themselves.
These are very simple rules.

June 27, 1993

Each soul has to be crowned by the *Dharma* of the self
And the *Dharma* of the self is the *praanas*,
which have been given to you and are yours.
When you stop wasting them on things which are
menial, inferior, or negative,
then all positive forces come and salute you.
These are certain laws which nobody can change.
That is why the Creator is bound by the
consciousness of the devotee.
People don't understand why [it is that we]
should we love each other.

May 6, 1996

The Soul and Infinity

Every Soul is God

Nobody even realizes that a soul lives in this body.

It is pure.

It is a gem.

It is clear.

It is God.

July 14, 1989

The fact is, soul is nowhere in us,

but soul is everywhere in us.

July 18, 1982

Soul is a part of the Universal Soul

called God.

June 30, 1985

Soul is not distinct from God.
Soul is God.

July 9, 1993

Man has a soul.
The soul is infinite.
Therefore, man can create action by the soul
that can be infinite.

July 10, 1994

Every soul is God.

June 27, 1996

The soul is not bound to your body.
Your body is bound to the soul.

July 12, 1983

Your soul is your God,
and it's right within you.
Your prayer is your only power,
and your grace is the only decoration you have.

July 18, 1994

A lot of disastrous things happen to people
when they get limited.
So, please
flow, grow, and glow.
Three words.
And keep going.
Wherever you shall be, understand
that God is not limited to a place or form.
Always rely on your soul.
That's the relationship -
you rely on your soul,
and God comes through.

July 29, 1994

Life has nothing more to it
than this chance -
to become truly divine
and truly a channel of God.

July 18, 1983

Life is to let it flow as God wants it to flow.

June 30, 1985

When people start serving the soul,
which is everywhere and nowhere,
they start becoming the soul.
The soul is a part of God.

July 18, 1982

Let God come through.

July 3, 1991

There is a soul and
all combinations of the soul is God and
everything that is life is God.

January 27, 1995

We are vibrating people.
We are perfectly imperfect
and imperfectly perfect.

June 30, 1983

The theory is that we have
the perfect God,
the noble God,
the divine God,
and that this noble and divine and perfect God
cannot create anything imperfect.
Therefore, in this universe there is nothing imperfect.
We may not know it, feel it, or understand it, but
everything is in balance.

July 27, 1983

Moment you start seeing God in you,
you will start seeing God in everybody.

March 8, 1996

Just accept yourself -
then you become divine
and God starts working for you.

September 29, 1993

Sometimes a person is so radiant and beautiful
that the One who is prayed to
comes and dwells within that person.
That is a universal merger of consciousness.

March 22, 1975

Receive and Manifest the Soul

Please remember that God is everywhere,
in every part of you,
but it has to be manifested.
Your soul is in every part of you,
in every tissue,
in every cell,
but it has to be received.
The purpose of life is to receive one's own soul.

July 18, 1983

God has to be manifested.
The soul has to be received and manifested.
For that, we have to prepare our body and mind.
That's why we have to have a discipline.
Now which discipline is true and which is not?
That's the question.
That discipline which makes us individual is not true.
That discipline which makes us Universal is true.

July 18, 1983

God is everywhere, but
God has to manifest.
You have to prove to other people that
you are more with God than with yourself.
That is the priority of the relationship with this planet.
Much happiness will come to you
if you can prove to people that
you are more with God than with yourself.

July 22, 1983

When you work on the self, you see your soul.
When you see your soul, you see the entirety of God.
What is above is below.
Whatever God is, that's what you are.
God is no different than you.

July 18, 1983

Relating to the Soul

You, the identity, and you, the soul,
when merged together,
God is experienced.

November 12, 1981

Relating to your spirit and soul
is relating to God within you.

August 27, 1992

You don't have a relationship with your soul.
Your soul has a relationship with you.
Because when you can look at
your spirit,
your soul,
your grit,
and your confidence,
then you are looking at God.

July 14, 1983

What is "soul aspect"?
Soul aspect is when man, in finite, relates to Infinity.
I don't care if you worship an idol.
I don't care if you worship a prophet.
I don't care what you are going to do.
But something you got to do,
yonder than you.
You must relate to some Infinity:
Jesus, Buddha, Mohammed, Ram!
Go ahead, doesn't bother me.

January 3, 1972

We always believe in one God,
but we have never found
our own oneness within our own soul,
the source of our own Godliness.
We have never seen
our own essential link to our own radiance,
that is our strength and our joy.

January 7, 1985

Go to your own soul for a change,
and make friends with it.
Talk to it.
Now, you will say how?
By Guru's word.
Between you and your soul,
the established communication is through Guru's words.
It is a bitter experience to sit calmly and read your *Banis*.
You don't want it, I know.
I never wanted it myself,
but it works.

July 10, 1988

How many of you have ever
gotten up in the morning with this idea?
"Let me connect with my soul.
Let me connect with my breath.
Let me connect with myself."

July 14, 1989

If you do not know your own soul,
you cannot reach any goal.

February 2, 1993

Sadness can only go away when your direction is towards God.
You are sad because you are not following your soul.
The strength of the soul is to go to God,
the strength of the mind is to know God, and
the strength of the body is to be God.

August 2, 1983

Now, the soul that you have is the same
as the dog has
and the cat has
and the tree has.
The structure of life is the same.
The tree has structure in which it grows,
I have structure,
and dogs grow in a structure, too.
We eat, live, sleep, and enjoy all in our own languages.
We have our own languages, communication, friendships,
societies, and worlds.
One thing is different -
And that is the consciousness to relate to Infinity.
Trees are under time.
Animals are under time with their mating season.
They are bound by time and space,
and you are not.
That is the only difference.

July 10, 1975

Do you ever consult your soul?

June 28, 1991

Caliber and consciousness, intelligence and intuition -
The soul is given these four things to complete the journey.
Emotion, feeling, fantasies, and irrationality
were given to destroy it.

June 27, 1996

The fact is, God is carrying you,
and you are carrying nothing.
It is the breath of life that is carrying you, and
it is the love of God that gives you the breath of life.
So what is the big deal?
Tomorrow will always be yours if you let it be.
If today has betrayed you,
you can always count on tomorrow.

June 30, 1983

To have the body is to have the *tattvas*.
To have the mind is to have the subtlety of Infinity.
To have the soul is to have you.
If you use the *tattvas* and the mind
to create friendship with the soul,
if you do your means and methods
to beautify your soul,
if you do all makeups and all planning
to shine your soul,
then you become God.
Who do you serve?
Do you serve your soul, or your mind, or your body?
Body and mind is given to you to serve the soul
and thus you can serve all that God is.
It's the simplest easiest way.
Don't love the shell so much.
Don't go for mussel so much that
you forget the pearl.

April 27, 1986

Soul and the Mind

Through the window of the mind,
you have to see the soul.
And through the sight
and the light of the soul,
you have to get initiated to see the Infinite Soul,
of which your soul is a part.

July 13, 1983

It is you who are against you.
What matters is what you say to yourself.
Conquer your mind with your soul.
Conquer your destiny with your soul.
Conquer your tomorrow with your soul.

June 23, 1997

Mind and soul are His alone.
What you say is,
"Soul is God's and mind is mine."
That's where the fight is.

March 8, 1987

Spirit is the Soul

When spirit is defined in a human being, it is called soul.
Soul, when it comes into the *praana* and *apaana* and
all the twelve *vayus*,
is known as spirit.

December 20, 1974

Spirit is God's will.
Spirit is not individual, and it will never be individual.

January 11, 1979

One thing which never changes in us is the spirit.
Otherwise, everything in us is finite, limited.

January 11, 1979

Spirit is the only Infinity
or source of Infinity in a human being.

January 11, 1979

Your spirit can expand and contract.

May 3, 1976

When somebody uses his ego,
he or she thinks it is the spirit.
My friends, ego and spirit are poles apart.
Ego is your limitation.
Spirit is your Infinity.

June 13, 1979

Spirit will never endanger you.
Spirit will exalt you.
Spirit will take you through every odd and end.
Spirit is your best guide.
Spirit is your best God.
Spirit is God in you.
Spirit flows through you, ego doesn't.
Though you require ego, you require ego as you require a car.
But you can't take a car into a living room.
When ego is stretched beyond its limit, it becomes a poison.
It becomes a dangerous species.
It totally ruins the individual.

June 13, 1979

To be spiritual is, without reservation,
to keep on wishing good.
Spirit is endless.
Spirit is endless and soul is endless.
To put it under the limitation of
good and bad is to defeat the purpose.

March 11, 1985

What Is the Soul?

Soul is a vibration.
Why are you still seeing the soul as a little ball?
I can read from your head
what you think about the soul.
What are you up to?
Don't imagine the soul is a ball.
Soul is a basic vibration.

October 14, 1971

What is a soul?
That is what I wanted to break in your imagination.
Soul is not a ball. It is a vibration…
It is just like this -
It's a frequency.
Let us talk that way.
All right, it is a unit frequency.
But it is always a pure self.
Basically, what you call a soul is a basic,
positive, unit frequency of the Totality.

October 14, 1971

Soul is what you call the mouthpiece.
The consolidated realm of the dance of the spirit is called soul.
Soul is the Being, and soul means that the Being is.
It is the flow of the spirit of Infinity into the finite.
The soul is the finite aspect of the Infinity.
It is a part of the Infinity.

August 21, 1978

What is the saint in you?
Don't you know that you are a saint?
The soul is your saint.

July 13, 1983

The guardian saint of your life is your soul.

July 13, 1983

Truth and the soul are not the same.
Truth is forever.
Soul is for a period.
Soul is a part of the truth that it has come to experience.
That's called a lifetime.

August 8, 1984

Why Have a Soul?

Have you ever understood
why the soul took the human body to begin with?
Just to eat? Soul doesn't eat.
Just to take bath? Soul doesn't bathe.
To have physical intercourse? Soul doesn't do intercourse.
What does the soul do?
Soul is a part of the Infinity, what you call God.
Soul seeks friendship with that Infinity, with that God.
It's a longing in us.
It's a feeling in us.

November 12, 1981

Without the soul, you cannot live.
You come here to live and experience,
that's why you got the soul.
You are part of God.
Soul is part of God.
You got this body and mind
to experience the creativity and the self of God in you.

July 18, 1983

Where is the soul?
The soul is everywhere in the body,
but you cannot pinpoint it.
You can pinpoint your heart, your lungs,
your kidneys, your head, and your brain.
You can understand the location
and function of everything.
But the soul, which is making everything function,
cannot be pinpointed.
It is, and it is not.
That's why the soul is God,
and God is the soul.

July 18, 1982

The soul is everywhere in the body
and still nowhere.
You will be everywhere
and still nowhere.
That is sainthood.
The men of God are everywhere and nowhere.
That is sainthood.

July 18, 1982

I am, I am,
because God wants to experience Himself.
The purpose of life is not me.
The purpose of life is my own Infinity.
That is why the soul is in me everywhere,
and still, I cannot locate it.
When Infinity is bordered or defined,
it becomes finite.
Because the soul is Infinity,
it is everywhere and nowhere.
God wants to experience Himself.

July 23, 1982

Without the soul, you cannot live.
You come here to live and experience.
That's why you got the soul.
You are part of God.
Soul is a part of God.
You got this body and mind
to experience
the creativity and the identity of God in you.

July 18, 1983

What is the idea of becoming pure?
To become pure and have God live in you
is an extremely selfish trip.
If the candle burns by itself, it is of no use;
but if the candle shows the path to others,
then the candle is worthwhile.
The idea of life is not to glorify yourself.
The idea of life is to glorify others.

July 18, 1983

A candle which does not burn
makes no difference to the darkness.
A person who does not share his higher caliber
makes no difference to the Kingdom of God.

July 17, 1983

God does not want those people
who work for themselves;
God wants those people
who work for God's entire kingdom.

July 18, 1983

By Giving you Become God

Giving is God
because only He gives
and takes nothing back.
And when somebody gives,
it is the Divine Consciousness
in essence
at that moment.

January 7, 1974

If you are not content with your own self,
don't even imagine anybody will be content with you.
If you don't love your own self,
how can someone love you?
If you don't have anything,
how can you share with anybody?
When you cannot give, you are not God;
and without giving, there is no God.

July 20, 1982

You are on this earth to experience
the ecstasy of consciousness
and live happily.
You are on this earth to live like God.
Give, give, give, give!
Give happiness.
Give joy.
Give people company.
Give smiles.
Give advice.
Uplift everybody.
You're their flow – the spirit in you.

January 1, 1983

Just start giving God to others.
Give God freely.
He will be around you all the time
because He knows you have no conditions of giving Him.
You give Him everywhere,
so, He will be there where you are,
everywhere.

February 5, 1989

What is the test of a Godly man?
A man who is humble,
who is sweet,
who is accommodating,
who is serviceful,
a man who smiles,
who is not upset,
a man who knows how to give
and not how to take.
This is what the God does.
God gives to you,
gives to you,
gives to you.
That is what God is.
And when He sits in you, you become all this.

April 23, 1969

So, God has many ways,
but God has only one way:
Those who give themselves to God
become God,
because originally, we all are part of God.

July 5, 1977

Remember,
this body comes from the Infinite,
and this being has an Infinite in it.
Therefore, relate to that infinite, blissful time
that is called life, and
succeed,
enjoy,
share,
give.
Give like God.
You will be in bliss.

January 8, 1985

Giving is God.
Taking is devil.
Give and give and give
and when it becomes hard for you to give,
then forgive and give.

November 15, 1983

Giving is God,
sharing is life,
and serving is Infinity of God.

January 8, 1985

Sometimes people give me presents.
I enjoy them,
because by giving, you become God.
By giving ego, you become God-people.
Ego is the barrier between becoming God and
remaining a human.
It was given to you for identification, and
whenever you speak from the consciousness of ego,
you speak from the earth,
and it is never beyond the third chakra.
But whenever you speak from the etheric level,
you are beautiful,
you are wonderful,
you are divine,
and God is with you.

July 12, 1979

Giving is giving and
giving is forgiving,
and forgiving is divine.

June 17, 1994

Whatever you give psychically,
electromagnetically,
through the communication,
through your vibration,
through your mental thoughts,
from the day of conception
to the one hundred and twentieth day,
to delivery,
is the foundation of the child.
Whatever in psyche,
in communication,
in trust,
in base you give a person,
is the person.
This cannot be denied.

July 10,1986

Giving is the art of life.
If you give, it will create a vacuum and God shall fill it.
But if you give and expect a return, you will get misery.
Then, what you give is a net loss.
I'll tell you the profit of loss and gain theory.
When you give, expect nothing.
Give from the heart, and you will get a hundred times in return.
I am telling you in the terms of western science.
The law of the vacuum is that there can be no vacuum.

January 29, 1985

Life is a personality of projectivity of positivity.
It has a character, and it has a commitment.
Whether you are human or you are animal.
You are what you can give.
You are not what you can take.

March 11, 1985

What is your attitude
when somebody is giving? Taking?
You have been trained that the opposite of giving is taking.
But that's the problem, you have to be retrained.
The opposite of giving is
gratefulness.
Whenever somebody gives,
be grateful.
If you don't want to be grateful,
don't take it.
Be grateful that somebody offered you something.
If [you think] giving can be balanced by taking,
you are totally neurotic, and
you are headed for ultimate ruin.

July 12, 1983

One who has merged
in the glory of God
shall not seek anything
from another human being.

July 21, 1977

Giving is giving.
It is always good to give
and keep on giving.
Don't get mad at those
who give you bad things
because,
after all,
they are givers, too.

March 5, 1985

Start Living Like Infinity

Listen to Infinity

We have to learn to listen
to that total creativity of divinity.

July 27, 1986

The test of discipline is
when you start living disciplined.
[Otherwise,] the mind starts going astray.
How do you win the mind?
When you do not care for the mind.
Only listen to the wisdom that suits your Infinity,
not to any other garbage.
When the mind gives you all the polarities
and you only listen to the reality,
that is Infinity.

October 16, 1978

What is the difference between a holy man and a non-holy man?
When a holy man talks or listens,
he talks from the fourth center,
and he listens through the fifth center.
The rest doesn't work. ...
He talks through compassion.
He listens to the projection of Infinity.

February 15, 1979

Do you know the power of listening to your own sound?
One who can listen to one's own sound
can listen to the entire infinity
of God.

February 8, 1994

If you develop yourself to listen,
the Infinite God shall listen to you.

February 10, 1989

Live in Grace

The purpose of this body is
to serve God's Grace.

July 18, 1983

Whatever positivity you can add to someone's life –
good deeds towards another …
That is living like God.

April 26, 1982

When you uplift others, God shall uplift you.
When you grace others, God shall grant you grace.
When you give to others, God shall give to you.

July 17, 1994

There is no God.

I am sitting in the presence of *Siri Guru Granth*,

I say it three times –

There is no God,

there is no God,

there is no God.

God is only when you are graceful.

Do not misrepresent yourself,

when you are graceful you are God –

There is God,

there is God,

there is God.

There is an ever-prevailing, almighty, everlasting God.

God only is with those who are graceful.

People who are not graceful

may talk about God.

They may do things about God,

but they have nothing to do with God.

There is no God in their realm of consciousness.

September 2, 1990

What do you mean by grace? ...
To act as God on earth.
Simple.
Your actions, your deeds, must prove
that you are God on earth.
But you must not say it.
You must not play it.
You must not pronounce it, nor announce it.
Just live it.

July 2, 1982

Live Like God

Live like God,
and fill people's heart
with love and peace.

August 10, 1975

You've got to live like gods.
You have to be universal.
You've got to go and serve people.
You have to spread among them,
And give them hope.
God will do the rest.

March 23, 1974

Accept God within you.
Be you,
and act with that consciousness.

July 16, 1989

You have to see God,
be God,
and look like God.

August 5, 1997

God created you.
Create God in yourself.
How?
Talk like God,
live like God,
and be like God.
Be as God made you.
Talk always in praise of the Lord
and live responsibly, thinking all the time –
God is with you.

May 17, 1978

Life is lived each day towards Infinity.
Therefore, it must be pointed towards Infinity.
It must be calculated that Infinity is known to me
and I am known to Infinity.
Stop finding.
Stop finding and start living.
Start living with Infinity.

August 14, 1978

If you believe in Jesus the Christ,
you must believe in what Jesus Christ believed.
Believing in Jesus Christ is not enough.
If you believe in Nanak,
then believe in what Nanak believed.
What is the proof that you believe?
You live it.
There is one way only to the One God,
and that one way is to live the Truth.
Knowing and believing the truth are not enough.
If you know the truth
and you believe the truth,
but do not live it,
you are called a hypocrite.
You know what a hypocrite is?
One who believes it, knows it,
and does not live it.

July 25, 1977

Live Your Spiritual Name

A spiritual *Name* is a calculated *Name*.
Once you get it,
you have to live by it.
It works both ways.
It is the destiny.
It is the goal that you must reach.
Spiritual *Name*s are not given to you
just to brand a bull or brand a sheep.
It is not a herd thing.
It's a mathematical calculation
in which you are told,
this is your destiny.
I mean, this is you.
You have to make it, too.
That's why we don't encourage [people to take a] spiritual *Name*.
People must ask.
So, when they ask,
they should know the responsibility.
They have to be ready
and they must live it.

July 29, 1978

We calculate it. It's a very simple formula.
The day you are born is the root of you,
genetically.
The longitude and latitude and the month
is the trunk of your tree,
and the year is your destiny.
So, we calculate.
We take the numerology
and add to it
and then take the number
and understand your cycle.

October 23, 1999

Spiritual *Name* is a *Name* of destiny
and the key of the procedural growth to reach Infinity.
Without Infinity,
finite is nothing.

August 14, 1978

Spiritual *Name*, in sound, relates to your *satva*.
It relates to your inner being, the truth.
The *Name* is computed in *Gurmukhi*.
Gurmukhi, which means "in the Guru's language",
also indicates your destiny.
That's what it means.
It is just like a flight plan to a pilot.
Do you understand?

August 23, 1981

When you call a person by the destiny-*Name*,
you pray for that person,
and that person is blessed by one prayer every time.
Your destiny-*Name* is the first step,
and it can help you reach your destiny.

March 8, 1983

Spiritual *Name* is called license, car license.
It is a spiritual vibration which, in human life,
you are supposed to adhere to
to reach God.
That's all,
no big deal.

April 3, 1985

Your spiritual *Name* is your destiny
and is the opposite of fate.
One who shall not live to their spiritual destiny,
which is the *Name*,
shall be taken away by their fate.
"IIn the beginning was the Word,
and the Word was with God,
and the Word was God."[4]
– and that is the *Name*.
God and devil,
fate or destiny,
heaven or hell
are just expressions.

February 13, 1985

---

4 John 1:1, New International Version Bible

Spiritual *Name* is the word.
Out of millions,
few get the chance even to claim it.
Try to understand the factuality of it.
Out of millions,
only few have the right to claim it.
And out of those who claim it, few shall live it.
But those who shall live to the word, oh Nanak,
shall be God on Earth.

February 13, 1985

If you can just live unto destiny and
let the destiny-*Name* be your *Name*,
you shall never have a defeat in your life.
If you put your energy towards destiny,
fate shall never touch you,
and you will live forever.

December 23, 1987

What is a spiritual *Name*?
Spiritual *Name* is the designated destiny
that becomes your identity,
rather than your identity on the earth.
Spiritual *Name* is a heavenly identity.
That's all it is.
You may not live up to it.
You may live up to it.
But it's the guiding force, and it's a prayer.
When somebody calls me, "Yogi Ji," this means
one who is united with the greatest soul.
Or somebody calls me, "Bhajan,"
it means a divine song.
And somebody calls me, "Harbhajan Singh,"
it means this lion who sings the divine song.
It's just a prayer.
It is prayers in another man's word.
It is a calling.
What is prayer?
It's a calling. That's it.
When you answer the calling,
you get uplifted.
It's a plus.
It's a way to get other people's blessings.
That's all.
It's no big deal.

April 22, 1990

Every soul has a root,
which is called *samskaras.*
Then, it has the orbit,
and then, it has the destiny.
We put three together and make up the spiritual *Name.*
Spiritual *Name* is a directive – your destiny.
You live up to it or not,
it's up to you.

December 10, 1990

You are God's incarnation on the earth.
If you live up to your spiritual *Name,*
the divinity, identity, social-self, and entire cosmos,
Prakriti and *Purkha*, will serve you.
Otherwise, you have to sweat.
That is the law of a spiritual *Name.*
When a person lives to their spiritual *Name,*
Prakriti and *Purkha* uplift that person as their child.
Those who do not live up to their spiritual *Name,*
they have to sweat.
Simple demarcation.

June 25, 1999

Your spiritual *Name* is,
at the longitude, latitude,
and the time and space you are born,
your journey of the soul,
your spirit.

July 15, 1992

Relate to God in All

Treat others as God.
You shall see God.

July 19, 1989

Those who shall serve others
with all their weaknesses and strength,
the Almighty God has no power but
to serve them.

June 20, 1993

A man of God is not offended.
He doesn't hate anybody because
somebody is fat,
somebody is thin,
somebody is rich,
somebody is not rich,
somebody is beautiful,
somebody is not beautiful.

April 23, 1969

If you start serving others and
see God in them,
you have reached the status of
God within you.

May 7, 1994

Help others,
and God shall help you.

December 31, 1996

Fo those who live a life where they can
see God in all,
the entire universe and Mother Nature
will uplift them and serve them,
and they shall have no death.

July 28, 1995

If you cannot see God in all,
you cannot see God at all.

August 19, 1995

I believe that you can give everything to all,
because that is the secret of God –
He gives it to all.

July 18, 1982

Relate to infinity

When you relate to Infinity,
you become part of Infinity.

March 28, 1972

Relate to Infinity,
receive it as Infinity,
and share it.
You will never be sorry.

January 8, 1985

How can you reach every heart and uplift it?
The theory is simple:
Relate to infinity.
Receive infinity and deliver it.

January 8, 1985

When the sun comes up, every son of God gets up,
including the daughter, indeed.
But those who get up earlier
in the very primal hour
can relate to Infinity
because their self, their ego,
is tuned into Infinity.

March 28, 1972

Speak like God

God is no secret, my friends.
God doesn't live anywhere,
God lives everywhere.
If you want to present God,
you can do it without any miracle.
Speak like God,
talk like God
and sing God's praise.

July 13, 1983

God is everything.
But when you speak like Him,
people misunderstand
and think you are God.

July 10, 1991

Praise the Lord.
When you praise the Lord,
you praise the inside of you.
Praising God is not doing anything to God.
God doesn't care.
You care.
It is your care.

July 17, 1994

Prayer is the Power

The power of prayer is when you talk to God.
Meditation is when God talks to you.

September 12, 1971

People of God pray, and God fulfills.
That is the relationship.
Relationship is not,
"Give me, give me, give me, give me."

July 9, 1975

Prayer is self-purification.

April 22, 1978

Prayer is nothing but cleaning the consciousness
so it can become radiant.

April 22, 1978

We don't mean what we say.
We say it as a ritual.
We talk phony –
Our words are phony.
We become phony,
and our prayer becomes phony.
That is why our prayers are not answered.

April 22, 1978

Prayer is tapping energy into my own unknown.
Whenever you want to reach your own unknown,
you do prayer.

July 21, 1982

The concept of prayer is to tap my own unknown for my known.
When known and unknown are united in oneness of the any self,
God is alive.
When known and unknown are separated in any concept,
God is dormant –
Not dead,
not gone.

July 21, 1982

Prayer is the power,
and power is the prayer.

July 13, 1983

Prayer opens you up when you feel you need help.

October 8, 1992

Prayer comes from within.
It is from the soul.

March 29, 1996

There is no other power on this earth
greater than the power
of prayer.

July 26, 1983

Defeat and victory are with God.
It's not with me.
It's not with you.
What we have is prayer.
We don't have any other power
but prayer.

June 29, 1986

Pray one minute a day
for peace.

June 23, 1997

Let us pray for
all mankind –
all peace,
all joy,
in all essence.

January 14, 1985

Just be kind.
Kindness is a continuous prayer
in itself.

August 4, 1983

Prayer is the power.

Power is not in the man.

Power is not in you.

You are not the power –

You never have been and you never will be.

Power is in the prayer.

Prayer is the projection.

Consolidated, concentrated projection is called prayer.

It is a one-pointed mind –

one-pointedness of being.

It comes from the very heart and spirit of the being,

and the head helps to put it together.

That's why when we pray, we bow our heads.

We kneel down and bend

because we want our heads to concentrate on our projection at that time.

Power is in the prayer.

There is no other power.

That's why Guru Nanak prayed,

and prayed,

and prayed.

July 12, 1983

The law is that where there is a known,
there is an Unknown.
If you continue relating to the known,
you are denying the Unknown.
If you relate to the known, which you are,
and you search out the Unknown,
that is a prayer.
You think you have to pray like this,
"Oh God, bless me."
No, it's totally unnatural.
God understands that you are folding the hands.
The power that is folding the hands
is God.
The lips that are uttering the prayer
is God.
The fact that you are trying to concentrate
is God.
You might be thinking, "I could have been eating pizza now."
Then you are making a posture of prayer.
Your mind is somewhere else.
You are somewhere different.
But when you are in tune with the Unknown,
the known is very peaceful.

July 14, 1982

When the mind is one-pointed towards the Divine,
you feel the Divine prevails through you.
That will happen when you pray for anything.
Remember,
conscious prayer to the Divine never,
ever goes unanswered.
And you cannot,
you cannot realize the Divine unconsciously.
You have to be conscious that the
Divine prevails through you.

March 30, 1971

You are a tremendous infinite power of Divine energy.
I have realized, it's ridiculous to feel,
"I can't."
There is no such thing as,
"I can't."
It doesn't exist.
It's man-made stuff.
Asking for sympathy/empathy is most ridiculous.
It is insulting and treacherous to be asking and praying for things.

October 29, 1992

Praying to God is ridiculous.
To be very honest with you,
it is ridiculous to pray to God.
It is ridiculous.
One of the most cheap things to say is,
"Oh mighty dear God."
He doesn't know hat is happening to you?
You believe that God does not know what's going on?
If you are that naïve
that you think He's such an idiot,
[do you think] that he's going to listen to you
when you talk to him?

July 14, 1975

Duality is Separation from Being One with God

So long as human consciousness,
in its conceptual projection
and objection,
does not understand
that there is but One God,
that there is nothing plural, two, about it,
then there is no redemption.
It is all corruption.

July 23, 1989

Duality is separation from being one with God.

July 23, 1989

Divinity is the oneness of which Guru Nanak wrote, *Eik Ong Kaar*.
Understand the simplicity in which God can
be experienced and seen,
strength and power can be gained,
neurosis and psychosis can be taken away,
by one simple attitude:
"I am, I am, I am God.
God within me is God.
God outside of me is God.
God around me is God.
All is God."
But, my God, your God, our God, their God, by God,
they don't know what God is.

July 23, 1989

You need to feed your soul,
and you will go wherever it can be nourished.
Your problem is, you are willing to feed your soul,
but you are afraid to commit to it.
That is your duality,
and you have to pay for it.

July 29, 1983

Eik Ong Kaar, the one within the One,
when it becomes one,
the One will be conquered,
and all will be conquered.
First conquer the One.
When you have a duality in you
and you are not one,
how can you reach the One?
How can two reach the One?
Understand the basic theory of God.
God is One.
You are one.
One you and one God merge to become
One.

November 27, 1984

Where there is Divinity, there is no duality.
Where there is a duality, there is no Divinity.

December 27, 1994

It may be hard at first for you to understand
how to be straightforward,
but if you really want to understand
the divinity of your own personality,
and, in reality, want to get rid of duality,
then you have to do a very simple act:
be straight.
You be you.

June 30, 1980

Those who are poor are the essential part of God.
Those who are rich are the essential part of God.
But when the rich man forgets that his richness belongs to God,
he is very, very poor.

January 7, 1985

How do you get to be divine?
Get rid of duality.
You will be divine.

December 27, 1994

God's Creation

I believe God couldn't do better
than to create us
as we are.

July 26, 1983

God is helpless in one way –
The perfect cannot create imperfection.

January 1, 1969

To accept God
is to accept the total creation of God.
To accept the total creation
and to accept God
requires *sadhana*.

July 5, 1981

God made you
what He made you.
He couldn't make it better,
couldn't make it worse.
If He could have,
He would have.

July 15, 1986

We have earned the *Karma*
to go through the ups and downs of life.
But now, if we have found God,
there is no need to give in.
Accept what God has given you
to keep going.

July 26, 1983

I believe God has created me

as a man

and if I keep myself

as a man,

God will keep me

as a man.

July 26, 1983

Evil holds the perception of the Divine.

If there's no evil,

how are you going to know

what is divine?

November 29, 1993

A personal God is absolutely a lie.

It is a bogosity.

It is a tragedy.

It is a human insanity.

It is a human psychotic, neurotic excuse

to kill, control, and connive.

When we become so terribly tragic that we make God personal,

that is the end of the road.

That is where humanity becomes bankrupt

of any consciousness.

God is a huge capacity of infinite, self-creative energy

that moves in a figure-eight shape.

It is unending.

It can never stop.

The figure eight has a circle above

representing heaven and

a circle below

representing the creation.

July 14, 1989

It is *ajoonee saibhang* –
never born, never dies, by Itself.
Anything which is by itself
is in absolute harmony.
When you are absolutely absolute,
you are absolutely in harmony.

July 14, 1989

There is a seen hand of God,
and there is an unseen hand of God.
Those who believe in the unseen hand of God
always get to see the seen hand of God at some time.
That is the bargain.
Those who don't believe in the unseen hand of God,
many times do not recognize
the seen hand of God.

July 17, 1983

You have been manufactured by God.
Every cell of your body has responsibility,
and your whole vibrations are controlled,
and you have [been] given over and above
the freedom to recognize your infinity within you.

Animals don't have that.
The difference between you and an animal is
only a simple difference.
It is a God creation. You are a God creation.
That is all right, and we agreed.
But its mind is limited.
Yours is unlimited.
That's the difference. ...

An animal cannot design the course of its life.
And whatever it designs, its course is limited.
You have no limits.
You can be anything.

February 10, 1972

A person, who through the bad times and good times
can maintain their grace
is always living <u>in</u> God –
and underline the word "in."

July 19, 1977

A man of God cannot do a lot of things.
But he can do one thing,
which is a most useful thing and worth doing.
He can change the strike of time.

In other words,
he can divert the energy from negative to positive.
That's all a man of God can do.
Because, he will never like to change the order of God.
When you love somebody, you will never like to
disobey that man.
So, if really he is a man of God,
he will not like to stand steadfast or stubborn.
No, this won't happen.
But he will divert the energy.

April 20, 1971

Lord God, give us the consciousness and awareness,
for our bad and good deeds
whatever we are,
as we are created in Thy image,
and we shall understand our *Satya*,
the truth, and the *Naam*, our identity.
May the truth and our identity be recognized by us,
so that we can uplift our self to Thy grace.
And may we keep up to Thy light,
to merge in Thine Infinity.
Sat Naam.

March 27, 1978

Kriyas and Meditations

Meditation to Achieve an Experience of God

August 22, 1986

Time: Start with 11 minutes and work up to 31 minutes.

Instructions:

1. Sit in Easy Pose.

2. Bend your elbows so that your upper arms are by your rib cage, and the hands are at shoulder level, palms facing forward. Bring each hand into Surya Mudra, with the thumb and sun finger (ring finger) touching. Keep the other three fingers straight.

3. Silently meditate to *Rakhe Rakhan Har* (by Singh Kaur).

Eyes Focus: Closed.

Mudra: Surya Mudra.

Mantra:

> *Rakhay rakhanahaar aap ubaarian,*
> *Gur kee pairee paa-ei kaaj savaarian,*
> *Hoaa aap dei-aal manaho na visaarian,*
> *Saadh janaa kai sang bhavajal taarian,*
> *Saakat nindak dusht khin maa-eh bidaarian,*
> *Tis saahib kee tayk naanak manai maa-eh,*
> *JJis simrat sukh ho-ei sagalay dookh jaa-eh.*[1]

Comments: Your hands are in Surya Mudra and you are meditating to a Surya Shabad. Let the surya (sun) energy circulate through your body. Close your eyes and go through your oneness.

---

1   From the Sikh prayer, *Rehraas Sahib*.

Meditation to Experience
You Are the Living God

December 20, 1974

Time: Not specified.

Instructions:

1. Sit in easy pose and grasp the hand of the person next to you. Let no hand be loose.

2. Close your eyes and go within following this visualization:

    "Meditate from top to bottom and feel that you are the living God. Lean on this one thought with all your energy. Don't worry what you were yesterday, day after, or many days before. No negativity is worth remembering. At this moment, concentrate fully and deeply and feel the ray of light of God in the universe enlightening you. [Feel] this tremendous energy descending upon you and making you radiant. Sincerely imagine that your constant effort and your sincere heart can create a miracle. Totally become a recipient and receive that tremendous energy and light. Feel totally enlightened as a living God. The purity of heart and the light of God will clean you clear and all your sins will depart.

    The grace of all people of God be with you. All their prayers be with you. All their blessings be with you. May you be filled with grace, light, and radiance. Receive, my dear ones, the blessing hand of God and radiate as the living God. Let your soul shine out of each pore of your life, through each fiber of your body, through each molecule and atom of your body. Let there be a tremendous light shining out. Fill yourself deeply with it and radiate through the vastness of the universe.

Make your mind to think nothing but the grace, nothing but the light, nothing but the radiance. Grow into the tremendousness of infinity. Inflate and become as great as total light. Cut yourself from every other thought. Wander not in any shallowness but instead, tune in into that greatness. Go within and expand out. Don't let your thoughts vary at this time. Receive and receive and shine out."

3. Begin chanting - *Sat Naam, Sat Naam, Sat Naam, Sat Naam, Sat Naam, Sat Naam, Wahe Guru*

4. Concentrate on your ears and you will hear the same sound.

Eyes Focus: Closed.

Mantra:

*Sat Naam, Sat Naam, Sat Naam, Sat Naam,
Sat Naam, Sat Naam, Wahe Guru*

Meditation to Break Nonreality

November 15, 1983

Time: 6½ minutes pranayama – 11 minutes chanting. 17½ minutes total.

Instructions:

1. Sit in easy pose with a straight spine.

2. Bend the elbows and raise the hands up and in until the heels of the hands meet in front of the heart.

3. Bring the hands in Lotus Mudra: touch the sides of the thumbs and the sides of the mercury fingers (little fingers) together. Let the other fingers be separated and slightly bent while point up to form the petals of a lotus.

4. Do the pranayama specified for 5 minutes.

5. After 6½ minutes of pranayama, chant for 11 minutes - *Har Jee, Har Har Har Har Har Jee.*

6. Repeat the pranayama for 5 minutes.

Eyes Focus: Eyes closed.

Mudra: Lotus Mudra.

Mantra:

Har Jee, Har Har Har Har Har Jee

Breath: Inhale normally (not too deeply) and hold. After 15-20 seconds, without exhaling, inhale more and hold. Again, after about 15 to 20 seconds, inhale more without exhaling and hold. Then, let the breath go. This is a triple inhale, and the breath is held in for a total of about 45 seconds. Rest for about 10 - 15 seconds and begin again.

Work up to a full minute breath cycle and eliminate the rest in between breaths as your lung capacity increases.

Comments:

"Make a lotus and balance the fingers in a such a way [that] the thumbs and the pinkies meet, with three [free] fingers just crossing the electromagnetic antenna – these three are my past, my present ,and my future. That's why three fingers are free. All three are free. [The other] two are the life connection– I was, I am, and I shall be. I am and I shall be are connected.

Close your eyes and look at what you are going to do. Inhale, hold. Inhale, hold. Inhale, hold. It is called triple inhale. You have to inhale thrice during one time of holding. Let it go, watch what happens. Inhale, hold, inhale, hold, inhale, hold, let it go, wow. Don't inhale too much when I say it the first time – a normal inhale, hold, inhale, hold, inhale, hold tight, let it go.

What this mantra tells you, in the sound of Naad Yoga, is that "God is, God is, God is, God is – Oh my soul, God is." It is a double affirmative used in the Naad.

The breathing and the lotus mudra we did was symbolic and effectively co-relative to the heart center. And the three-breath ... [affects] the pressure meridian of the heart center. If you scientifically do that, in about ninety days you will totally find a change of your behavior. What does it do? It is fantastic. That is the only word I can use. You will like it."

Meditation for
Christ Consciousness

March 22, 1976

Time: Start with 11 minutes.

Instructions:

1. Sit in easy pose with your spine straight.

2. Place the thumb of each hand on the mound below the mercury finger (little finger). Press your palms together so that the right thumb fits nicely on top of your left thumb. The thumbs are parallel and put enough pressure that the moon area, the mound below the thumb, is pressed together. It is a little tricky to get a perfect fit. Make sure your hands are pressed firmly together so that the bottom of the palms (moon area) are touching.

3. The hands are held at the diaphragm level, pointing slightly upward.

4. Inhale completely while mentally repeating the mantra once. Then hold the breath for 16 repetitions and exhale with one more repetition. Thus, there is a total of 18 mentally vibrated mantras. The inhale should take about five seconds, the held breath 20-25 seconds, and the exhale about five seconds.

Eyes Focus: Not specified.

Mantra: Any mantra that inspires you to Infinity. Wahe Guru, or Sat Naam is a good example.

To End: Drink water after the kriya.

Comments:

"When you do this meditation, the order is you should wait for few minutes and then drink a glass of water or some liquid. Start with about 11 minutes. ...There is a very classic situation where you can inhale, taking about five seconds to inhale, then you take about twenty to twenty-five seconds to hold the breath, and five seconds to let the breath go. You will find tremendous energy in you. Tremendous energy. That's why the requirement is when you finish it, drink some tea. In Tibet, when they do it, they take butter tea and drink it. In India they drink milk, but in the West water will do.

According to the written records, which I found in Kashmir there was a man Yesu – they call him Jesus in the West. Yesu Hazareth, Yesu of Nazareth, a carpenter – in West you call him Jesus Christ of Nazareth. He used to talk and when he used to come into ecstasy, he'd praise the Lord. There is no mantra given with it, but the meditation is there."

Meditation to Connect Up to Infinity

January 11, 2000

Time: 28 minutes, 10 minutes, 4 minutes, 3 minutes. 45 minutes total.

Instructions:

1.   Sit in easy pose.

2.   **Part One**:

   a.   Right hand is held up beside the right shoulder with the elbow relaxed down. Lock the first two fingers close together pointing upwards and use the thumb to hold the other two.

   b.   Left hand rests at your Heart Center.

   c.   Eyes closed.

   d.   Chant from the navel *Ong Namo Guroo Dayv Namo* (*Ong Namo Guru Dev Namo* by Nirinjan Kaur) for 28 minutes.

   e.   **To end** – Inhale deeply, hold 10-15 seconds, exhale like cannon fire through the nostrils. Repeat two more times.

3. **Part Two**:

   a. Same posture, but switch hands with the left hand up and the right hand at the Heart Center.

   b. Chant from the navel, *Whaa-hay Guroo, Whaa-hay Guroo, Whaa-hay Guroo, Whaa-hay Jeeo* (*Wahe Guru, Wahe Jio* by Sangeet Kaur and Harjinder Singh Gill from *Raaga Sadhana*) for 10 minutes. Divide into three parts: First part aloud (about 3.5 minutes), second part in a strong whisper from the navel (about 4.5 minutes), third part in deep silence (about 2 minutes).

4. **Part Three:**

   a. Same posture.

   b. Chant from the navel *Sat Naaraa-ein Whaa-hay Guroo, Haree Naaraa-ein Sat Naam* (*Sat Narayan Wahe Guru, Hari Narayan Sat Nam* by Snatam Kaur) for 2.5 minutes.

   c. Chant with *bekhri* (with the tip of the tongue), from the navel center.

   d. Continue chanting and bring the hands to the heart center in prayer pose for another 1.5 minutes.

5. **Part Four:**

   a. Hands in prayer pose, chant from the navel for 3 mins:

   > *Har Har Har Har Gobinday,*
   > *Har Har Har Har Mukanday,*
   > *Har Har Har Har Udhaaray,*
   > *Har Har Har Har Apaaray,*
   > *Har Har Har Har Haree-ang,*
   > *Har Har Har Har Karee-ang,*
   > *Har Har Har Har Nirnaamay,*
   > *Har Har Har Har Akaamay*
   > (*Har Har Har Har Gobinday* by Nirinjan Kaur).

   b. **To end:** Inhale, exhale, relax.

Eyes Focus: Eyes closed.

Mantra:

1. **Part One:**

   Ong Namo Guroo Dayv Namo

2. **Part Two:**

   Whaa-hay Guroo, Whaa-hay Guroo, Whaa-hay Guroo, Whaa-hay Jeeo

3. **Part Three:**

   Sat Naaraa-ein Whaa-hay Guroo, Haree Naaraa-ein Sat Naam

4. **Part Four:**

Har Har Har Har Gobinday,
Har Har Har Har Mukanday,
Har Har Har Har Udhaaray,
Har Har Har Har Apaaray,
Har Har Har Har Haree-ang,
Har Har Har Har Karee-ang,
Har Har Har Har Nirnaamay,
Har Har Har Har Akaamay[2].

Comments:

About the silence in part two:

"Go deep into the silence. In silence you speak in yourself, and you must hear it by your ears. That will give the power to hear the unknown sounds of the world. You can talk with birds, and animals, and humans alike. Get deep into the silence. Do not bend your spine. Be alert."

About the mantra in part four:

"This is called the *Guru Gaitri*. Solitarily and relaxed, it has eight words only. *Gobinday, Mukanday, Udhaaray, Apaaray, Haree-ang, Karee-ang, Nirnaamay, Akaamay* – eight words. We add Har four times to [each line and the] total becomes 40. 40 is a four-double-zero that's a "cup of prayer." And 40 is half of 80. Eight is Infinity. If God doesn't happen to bless you, the question is not who you are, the question is what do you project? The question is not what you control, the question is, 'Do you have self-control?'."

---

2   From the Sikh prayer by Guru Gobind Singh, *Jaap Sahib*.

CONNECT THE FINITE IDENTITY WITH THE INFINITE IDENTITY:
Meditation Into Being: I am I am

April 7, 1972

Time: 11 – 31 minutes.

Instructions:

1. Sit in an Easy Pose, with a light *Jalandhar* bandh.

2. Keep the spine straight. Place the right hand over the right knee. Keep the elbow straight and the hand relaxed in *Gyan Mudra* (the index finger tip on the tip of the thumb).

3. Raise the left hand in front of the Heart Center. The palm is flat and faces toward the chest. The fingers point to the right.

4. Start with the left hand 6 inches (15 cm) from the chest. Chant out loud "I Am" as you draw the hand closer to the chest to a distance of about 4 inches (10 cm).

5. Then chant "I Am" as you extend the palm straight away from the front of the chest to a distance of about 12 inches (30 cm).

6.   Then take a short breath through the nose as you draw the hand back to the original position of 6 inches (15 cm) from the chest.

7.   Create a steady rhythm with the mantra and the breath.

Eyes Focus: Eyes are 1/10th open, with the eyes looking straight forward through the eyelids.

Mantra: *I am. I am.*

To End: Inhale deeply, hold, and relax completely.

Comments:

This mantra connects the finite and Infinite identities. The first "I Am" that emphasizes the "I" is the personal and finite sense of self. The second "I Am" that emphasizes slightly the "Am" is the impersonal and transcendent sense of the Self. All real mantras blend this polarity of the Infinite and finite in their internal structure and design. If you only say the first "I Am", the mind will automatically try to answer, "I am what?" This sends the mind on a search through all the categories and roles that hold the finite identities. If you immediately say the second part of the mantra, "I Am" the thought becomes "I Am what I Am". To be what you are is the essence of truth and will lead you to the nature of Reality. The hand and the breath move in rhythm and strengthen your ability to maintain a sense of self as your awareness expands. A yogi cultivates the relationship between the finite sense of the self and the Infinite sense of the Self. The mind often forgets this relationship when it becomes attached to a particular emotion or object that it wants to keep. One of the important habits the yogi instills in the mind is the ability to break that trance of attachment by a shift to the perspective of Infinity. This is also the perspective of Being. You exist before the objects you collect and even before the body that you use. It is very powerful and effective to remind the mind of your true identity with your Infinite Being. Without this awareness, then philosophy, ethics, and spirituality will reduce to ritual participation in the "good." What the yogi seeks is to participate in life with authenticity and wholeness.

Meditation to Conquer Self-denial

April 3, 2001

Time: 31 minutes.

Instructions:

1. Sit in easy pose with a straight spine.

2. Bring both hands in prayer pose in front of the throat center. Slide the left hand up so that the fingertips of the right hand fit exactly on the mounds of the left palm. The fingertips of the left hand are at the level of the 3rd eye. Elbows are relaxed down.

3. Close the eyes and chant from the navel. Nirinjan Kaur's recording of:

Har Har Har Har Gobinday,
Har Har Har Har Mukanday,
Har Har Har Har Udhaaray,
Har Har Har Har Apaaray,
Har Har Har Har Haree-ang,
Har Har Har Har Karee-ang,
Har Har Har Har Nirnaamay,
Har Har Har Har Akaamay

Eyes Focus: Eyes closed.

To End:

*   Inhale deeply, hold approximately 15 seconds, exhale.

*   Inhale deeply, hold approximately 15 seconds, and apply total pressure to where the fingertips meet the mounds of the hand, exhale.

*   Inhale deeply, hold approximately 20 seconds and press hard on the fingertips, equalizing the energy with all your force. Exhale and relax.

Comments:

This meditation will help you be delightful. The strength of your mind will increase many times.

Meditation for Divine Grace – Gum Kriya

May 29, 1980

Time: May be practiced 5 to 31 minutes.

Instructions:

1. Sit in easy pose with a straight spine.

2. Make a fist with the left hand and wrap the right hand around it. If you are right-handed cross the left thumb over right; if you are left-handed reverse the thumbs, right over left.

3. With arms relaxed and elbows bent, raise the hands in front of the chest at heart level.

4. The Heart Lock is held comfortably with the right hand squeezing the left.

5. Inhale deep, chant the mantra 5 times in one breath -
   Sat Naaraa-ein Whaa-hay Guroo, Haree Naaraa-ein Sat Naam.

Eyes Focus: Eyes are closed.

Mantra:

Sat Naaraa-ein Whaa-hay Guroo, Haree Naaraa-ein Sat Naam.

"[It is a] two and half cycle [mantra and] you have to be totally systematic, otherwise you will either repeat it six times or you will stop at the fourth time. The trick is in that fifth turn."

Comments:

"When you are emotional or commotional, it only means you are trying to force your way. When you use force, it will naturally have the reaction of force. Force gets the reaction of force. Action must respond to reaction. If you are not ready for reaction or you do not want reaction, start communication. That's the law of communication. The essence of communication is you must communicate with yourself so that you know yourself, you understand yourself, you feel yourself and from that place of knowing, you can communicate with everybody, all selves.

If you correctly [repeat the mantra] five times within one breath, in that posture, it can totally let you feel Divine Grace. It is sometimes called Panch Kriya, also. It's a very beautiful kriya. It will take you time to understand it and to practice it. It requires lot of practice, but if you practice this one, it will be a lot of fun. ... It is the best way to become disease free."

Elevate the Self Beyond Duality

April 26, 1976

Time: Begin with 5½ minutes and slowly work up to 31 minutes. 31 minutes of this meditation can keep you in a very elevated state.

Instructions:

1. Sit in a comfortable meditative posture.

2. Lift your hands to the level of your heart, palms up, elbows relaxed by your sides.

3. Form a shallow cup of your hands by placing the side of your hands together from the base of the palms to the tips of the Mercury fingers (pinkies). The fingers of each hand are held together (touching) but not rigidly. The thumbs are relaxed away from the fingers. The cup is shallow, the edges of the cup are about thirty degrees up from the parallel plane. It is important to keep the "line

of Mercury" connected; the outsides of the hands touch from the Mercury fingers to the base of the palms. Normally, there will be no opening whatsoever, but some people will have a gap between their little fingers. Keep this gap to a minimum.

4. Close your eyes and look into your hands through your closed eyelids.

5. Chant *Ik Ong Kaar, Satigur Prasaad* in a monotone voice. One repetition of the mantra takes between three to four seconds.

Eyes Focus: Eyes closed looking into your hands through closed eyelids

Mantra:

   Ik Ong Kaar, Satigur Prasaad

Comments:

"Ik Ong Kaar, Sat Gur Prasaad is the most powerful and potent mantra of all the mantras. There is nothing equal to it, nor anything that can explain it. *Ik Ong Kaar, Sat Gur Prasaad* is a *Pritam* Mantra, the entire Siri Guru Granth Sahib is nothing but an explanation of this one mantra. Its combination is so strong that when you do the *Japa*, (repetition of) *Ik Ong Kaar, Sat Gur Prasaad,* it elevates the self beyond duality, and it establishes the flow of the spirit. If you meditate on it, it will make the mind so powerful that it will remove all obstacles and establish the flow of the spirit. We also call it a "magic mantra" because its effect is soon and positive and very durable. Therefore, please remember ...that it has to be chanted in a place of reverence and with reverence. When you meditate on this mantra, see to it that the place and the surrounding has a serenity in reverence and that you do it with a reverence...

"I would like to give you a basic warning. It is not secret but it is very sacred, so chant it with a reverence, write it with a reverence, and use it with a reverence. Normally, we were told when you start meditating with this mantra, chant to God first. Either chant one *Mool Mantra*:

Ik Ong Kaar, Sat Naam, Kartaa Purakh, Nirbhau, Nirvair, Akaal Moorat, Ajoonee Saibhang, Gurprasaad, Jaap, Aad Sach, Jugaad Sach, Hai Bhee Sach, Naanak Hosee Bhee Sach.

Or the Mangala Charan [of *Sukhmani Sahib*]:

Aad Guray Nameh, Jugaad Guray Nameh, Sat Guray Nameh Siree Gurdayv ay Nameh.

Or some other mantra before it just to purify and then [start.]"

Meditation to Expand the Ego to the Extent that You Are the Universe

January 26, 1973

Time: Not Specified

Instructions:

1. Sit down in a posture, which is convenient to body with your spine as straight as possible. It must be graceful. That is the first requirement that your posture should be graceful, steady, and convenient.

2. Close your eyes and go within. Your eyes must [close to] open your inner eye. Outer eyes must not see.

Visualization:

"Now start imagining that you are the greatest self-enlightened being. You are great, great, great, great, great, great, great, great, great, great, whatever it is, totally and perfectly enlightened being.

"Your body can be still at your command. Your nose is still under your supervision. Your thoughts are under your [control]...

"You are mentally, physically, spiritually, totally a being who knows all about everything. You shall not limit your thinking about greatness. Get all the thought from the intuitive mind and the intellect should leave those thoughts in you, and flood yourself that you are the greatest. You are the master of universe and expand your ego to the extent that you are the universe. You are the Infinite One. You are the Being of the beings, Supreme Being. ...

"A lot of negative thought will cross you but you cross all of them. Keep on growing. Whosoever has brought you here, has brought you here for growth. All He wanted was for you to be here, to find a place. Growth is always His, then He will take care of your mental growth and your levitated form as a being. Dedicatedly transfer yourself into the hands of the Being, to be the Supreme Being, by yourself."

Eyes Focus: Closed.

Meditation to Experience the Infinity of God

November 09, 1998

Time: 9.5 minutes, 3 minutes, 9.5 minutes. 22 minutes total.

Instructions:

<u>**Part One**</u> – 9½ minutes

1. Sit in easy pose.

2. Raise the right hand with the elbow
    relaxed at the side and the hand at
    shoulder level palm facing forward.
    Make a fist and extend only the
    Jupiter finger (index finger) pointing
    up while the rest of the hand
    remains in a fist. Place the left hand
    over the heart center with the fingers
    together and pointing to the right.

3. With a deep, long whistle in through
    the mouth, raise the Saturn finger
    (middle finger) up, resulting in two
    fingers pointing up. Exhale deep,
    long through the nose and lower
    the Saturn finger back to the fist.
    "Use your breath and see the system
    works. You are making your brain cells
    remodel themselves."

4. Breath powerfully

5. Without pause, go to the next part.

Part Two – 3 minutes

1. Raise your arms 4 to 6 inches over the top of your head and interlace your fingers with the thumbs relaxed apart.

2. Drink air in through the mouth and exhale through the nose. Inhale like you are drinking water.

3. Without pause, go to the next part.

Comments:

"Wet air goes in so that you burn out all that you have in your mind. Feel clear. Feel healthy. Use your own prana to give yourself confidence. You have your own arc line and aura, and just get deeply involved for a few minutes. Concentrate on your heart center. Drink air deeply and let it go through the nostrils. The armpits are the exhaust pipe of the brain – this will have a new meaning when you are finished! Mechanically breathe in and powerfully breathe out."

Part Three – 9½ minutes

1. Bring both hands to your heart center, with the right hand under the left hand.

2. Close your eyes and breathe long, deep and absolutely slow.

Comments:

"Breathe long, deep, and slow and please find God as a deity sitting in your heart center as you hold it with both hands. Every request within yourself, all expansion, you within you, all prosperity, you within you shall come to you if you pray to the Lord, holding Him with your own hands, you unto you, at the heart center. Feel no weakness, being one to one, face to face. Every finite has the authority and blessing and goodwill to face the Infinity.

"When you hold your heart with a presiding deity of that Infinity, the sound word is 'Whaa-Hay-Guroo,' the *Trikuti* - Father, Son, and Holy Ghost, all in one's self. You breathe long and deep and love your *prana*, love the breath of life. You shall find results.

"Be careful - your physical system may do some short circuiting or your mind may flip little bit, but you are the one who commands to hold it. This is the most precious prayer and moment of your life...Make yourself stronger and stronger and stronger.

"The deeper the breath, better the result....Spread your rib cage to the maximum. Bring up a lot of prana to your heart center. Let it be lit by your own grace...Long, deep inhale will burn the disease in the deepest corners of your lungs and your body. Letting God preside in you with His presence at your heart center. It's the most wonderful and beautiful moment of your life when you as a finite can understand Infinity within you. Feel it, touch it and relate to it."

To End:

Inhale deeply and cross your arms across your chest, holding opposite elbows with your hands. With the strength of the locked elbow squeeze your body in every fiber and hold the breath tight. Push hard so your digestive system can recuperate and be cured. Hold tight for 20 seconds, cannon fire out.

Inhale again, as deeply as you can, and squeeze the entire body. With the help of the elbow lock, distribute the energy into every part of the body. Hold tight for 10 seconds, cannon fire out.

Inhale again, as deeply as you can, and squeeze the entire body. Hold tight for 20 seconds and relax.

Comments:

"Have you ever gotten the idea that you are bigger and higher than you are? If you ever think you are bigger and higher than you are, you will not be lying. You will not have to and you don't have to prove it to anybody. Then, what will happen? You will have *Vakh Siddhi* – whatever you say, doesn't matter what it is, shall happen. Five tattvas shall manifest it and that's how humans are going to live in their ecstasy of consciousness.

"Beauty is in the heart. Somebody asked me today, "What should I do?" I said, "Do nothing. Just think, God lives in Heart Chakra. Make it a shrine. Do whatever you are doing, I am not discussing it. Just make a shrine in your heart for God to live. Just remember that.

"We have to cross this age. We are not born to suffer. We are not subject to anybody. God made me, made you and made us, and He made it all with equal affection. The Almighty Lord, the best of all, the greatest of all, the perfect of all, could not create anything imperfect. You may look imperfect to yourself. But in the eyes of God, you have already earned it. You are here to do what? To see the Infinity of God, to experience the Infinity of God."

Meditation to Experience Your Totality, Reality, Infinity

August 27, 1991

Time: 5 minutes and 8½ minutes. 13½ minutes total.

Instructions:

Part One – 5 minutes

1. Sit in easy pose with a straight spine.

2. Touch the tip of the thumb to the tips of the Saturn and Sun finger. (Thumb to middle and ring fingers.)

3. Stretch the arms out in front of your body, parallel to the floor creating a 90 degree angle between them.

4. Lock the chin in tight and stretch the shoulders out. With the strength of the arms, stretch so you gain about an inch in length. The armpits, which are the center of the nervous system, will be activated.

5. Eyes gaze down at the tip of the nose.

6. Sing with the mantra *Ang Sang Whaa-hay Guroo* ("*Ang Sang Wahe Guru*" by Nirinjan Kaur).

240

To End: Inhale deeply and hold. Lock the neck tight, stretch your arms from the shoulders, and pull your armpits open for about 20 seconds. Exhale. Repeat two more times.

Part Two – 8½ minutes

1. Bring your hands down into your lap and relax.

2. Keep the eyes closed.

3. Breath very deeply and extremely slowly, and let the energy flow. "Breathe the fragrance of the prana."

4. After 3½ minutes, Listen to the song "Flowers in the Rain" (by Gurdass Singh). Breathe the fragrance of the praana, slowly and very deeply.

To End: Inhale deep. Suspend the breath for about 20 seconds. "Love it, feel it, experience it. And give it a prayer to make you healthy, happy and holy, let it go."

Breathe again. Suspend the breath for about 25 seconds. "Know it, feel it, experience it, understand it. And do a prayer which will make you healthy, happy and holy. Let it go."

Breathe again. Suspend the breath tightly for about 40 seconds. "With the power of the breath, experience your whole being, experience your whole being, experience your whole being, thirty trillion dancing Gods in you. Experience the beautiful, bountiful light. Experience your totality, reality and your Infinity. Feel it, feel it, experience it, experience it, experience it. And out of that joy let it go."

Meditation to Extend the Brain to Infinity, also called Meditation for Stress or Sudden Shock

January 29, 1979

Time: In this class, the meditation was taught for 4½ minutes with a warning to slowly build up the time, not to exceed 31 minutes.

Instructions:

1.   Sit straight in a comfortable position with a straight spine.

2.   Relax the arms down with the elbows bent. Moving from the elbows draw the forearms in toward each other until the hands meet in front of the body about 1 inch above the navel.

3.   With both palms facing up, rest the right hand in the palm of the left hand. Press thumb-tips together and pull the thumbs toward the body.

4.   Inhale deeply. Chant the mantra in a monotone as the breath is completely exhaled *Sat Naam Sat Naam Sat Naam Sat Naam Sat Naam Sat Naam Whaa-hay Guroo.*

5.   Each word is one beat. The entire mantra is chanted on one breath. Use the tip of the tongue to pronounce each word exactly.

Eyes Focus: Look at the tip of the nose.

To End: Inhale deeply, hold the breath and stretch the arms up over the head as high as possible. Stretch with every ounce that you can muster. Exhale and relax down. Repeat 2 more times.

Comments:

This meditation balances the left hemisphere of the brain with the base of the right hemisphere. This enables the brain to maintain its equilibrium under stress or sudden shock. It also keeps the nerves from being shattered under those circumstances.

When your prayer does not work and nothing else seems to work, practice this meditation and see how quick it WILL work. The rhythm is unique and must be maintained. This meditation causes the heavy area of the vagus nerve to activate. This extends the brain, eventually to Infinity. The result for the meditator is that he will blossom into his entire potential.

Meditation to Direct Your Fear to Motivate You to Infinity

October 30, 1978

Time: In class, the meditation was for 17 minutes. Begin with 11 minutes and slowly build the time to 31 minutes.

Instructions:

1. Sit in a comfortable position.

2. Bend the elbows with forearms parallel to the ground and bring the hands in front of the Heart Center.

3. Right hand palm up pointing to the left and left hand palm down pointing to the right.

4. The right hand is just above the left, hands are parallel to each other and the ground.

5. The fingers of each hand are side by side touching.

6. Bend the neck and lock the chin down against the chest.

7. Inhale deeply and completely exhale three times.

8. Then, start the timer, and inhale and chant the mantra three times on each breath.

Eyes Focus: Tip of the nose.

Mantra:

> *Aad Sach, Jugaad Sach, Hai Bhee Sach,*
> *Naanak Hosee Bhee Sach*

End: Inhale, hold 15 seconds and exhale. Repeat two more times.

Comments:

"This meditation directs your fear towards motivating you to Infinity. It will bring a simple polarity to your own magnetic field. Anything that has been neutralized and is weak, this meditation will make strong.

"You want to live life, [then] live a committed life. This is the price you pay. There is no freedom that is free. There is no liberty without labor... Fear should motivate [you] towards Infinity."

Meditation to Feel Free from Attachment to the Earth and Give God a Chance

July 14, 1998

Time: 13 minutes.

Instructions:

1. Sit in a comfortable position.

2. Bring your hands together in front of your chin with fingers pointing up, palm and fingers not touching except for the tips. The point where the tip of the Saturn (middle) fingers touch is about six inches from your nose.

3. Chant with Nirinjan Kaur's recording of *"Har Har Har Har Gobinday."*

4. At every *"Har,"* press all five fingers together. Create equal meridian pressure in the finger tips when you press.

5. After 10 minutes, begin whistling the mantra instead of chanting. Continue for the last 3 minutes.

Eyes Focus: Focus on the tip of the nose.

Mantra:

Har Har Har Har Gobinday,
Har Har Har Har Mukanday,
Har Har Har Har Udhaaray,
Har Har Har Har Apaaray,
Har Har Har Har Haree-ang,
Har Har Har Har Karee-ang,
Har Har Har Har Nirnaamay,
Har Har Har Har Akaamay.

To End: Inhale, inhale very deeply. Hold it. See yourself as a conscious being and whistle out with a complete exhale. Whistle out to the last bit of breath. Inhale and hold it. Whistle out. Inhale deeply again, hold it and put all your pressure on the tip of fingers and bring the whole body into synchronization. Exhale with cannon fire out. Relax.

Comments:

"If you are alert and you know your boundaries, you know your conception, you know your projection, you know how to move, you have all the manners, you have the commitment and the character, nobody can touch you. I am not saying they will not try, they will, but they won't go anywhere. Especially a woman who is not flexible, alert, well-disciplined and cannot confront the passage of life with her total dignity, will end up in pain... A person who gets rid of shallowness and claims courage, is compassionate and straightforward. There is no power on the Earth that can make them poor or undermine them."

Meditation to Feel God Within You

June 22, 2001

Time: 3 minutes, 11 minutes. 14 minutes total.

Instructions:

Part One

1. Sit in a comfortable position with a straight spine.

2. Place cupped hands over your ears with the fingers pointing to the back.

3. Chant for 3 minutes from the navel in a monotone: "God and me, me and God, are One."

4. **To End** – Maintain your hands over your ears. Inhale deep and hold as long as you can - chin in and chest out stretch your spine up. Exhale. Repeat two more times.

Part Two

1. Remaining in the posture and immediately begin to chant from the navel, *Hamee Ham Brahm Ham* ("*Humee Hum*" by Nirinjan Kaur).

2. Concentrate on the navel and enjoy the result. Feel God within you.

3. Continue for 11 minutes.

4. **To End** – Inhale deeply, hold 10-15 seconds, stretch your spine and press your ears putting the maximum pressure on the ears. Repeat two more times. Relax.

Comments:

"At this time, we should make a sincere promise - you will shine. All problems, will be taken care of. Every day, I see God working for me, I have forgotten to work. I see God using me as an instrument. Nobody recognizes this. Time will recognize it. Just think how people will look at me a thousand years from now. Think of it. You know what they look at me for? The man who came and survived in the most passionate storm of the United States and carried the flag of consciousness [to the] world at large. He was grateful for His kindness, and he led the path away from drugs, commotions and nonsense...

"So what have I done? I have done my job. I have created something and I have allowed people to participate in everything, so that your tomorrow may not look alien to you. I have given you, Bana, Bani, Seva, Simran – the four aspects of life, so you can be recognized, you can serve, you can be, and you can be pure. It's the subjective purity in you that shall achieve the objectivity of life. It's a simple bargain.

"You love me, I know. But when I am gone, you will miss me, that I also know. But that will be a misunderstanding, [because] I'll be within you. That's how consciousness multiplies. The body has to drop. [The] body has to drop, no matter what. But it multiplies into the being. You may not feel it for the time being, but you will know it. It's a fact. There is no claim to it. It is the unseen hand of God that does it. It has been happening for centuries, and it will continue to happen…Neither be fanatic nor be lazy, nor egomaniac, nor crazy. Just be. Learn to tolerate criticism. Learn to tolerate abusiveness. Do you know how much pain [the person abusing you is in?] …You are needed. That's why God brought you here - to give you the experience."

Meditation Grace of God –
for Women

Instructions:

<u>Part One</u>

1. Lie on the back, fully relaxing the face and the body.

2. Inhale deeply, hold the breath in while silently repeating
    the mantra 10 times. Tense the fingers one at a time to keep
    count. Exhale all the air out, hold it out and silently repeat the
    mantra 10 times. Continue this process of repeating the mantra
    10 times on each inhale and 10 times on each exhale, for a
    total of 5 inhalations and 5 exhalations. This totals 100 silent
    repetitions.

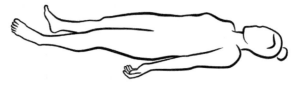

Part Two

1. Relax your breath, and with eyes still closed, slowly come
    sitting up into Easy Pose.

2. Bring the right hand into *Gyan Mudra*, resting on the knee. The
    left hand is held up at the level of the left shoulder, palm flat
    and facing forward, as if you are taking an oath.

3. Keep the breath relaxed and normal. Tense only one finger of the left hand at a time, keeping the other fingers straight but relaxed. Meditate on the governing energy of each finger (see table), then repeat the mantra aloud 5 times. Beginning with the Mercury Finger, continue this sequence for each of the remaining fingers, finishing with the thumb. This totals 25 repetitions.

Eyes Focus: Eyes closed.

Mantra:

I Am Grace of God

To End: Inhale, exhale. Relax and meditate silently for a few minutes.

Comments:

It is said that when a woman practices this meditation for one year, her aura will become tipped with gold or silver, and great strength and God's healing powers will flow through her. Positive affirmation is an age-old technology. Words increase in power through repetition, and when you are repeating truth, the impact is enormous. This is one of the most powerful affirmations a woman can do. The fact is, woman is the Grace of God. Woman is Shakti. The problem is, she doesn't know it.

This meditation is designed to evoke and manifest the inner grace, strength, and radiance of each woman. It helps her to tune in directly with the Adi Shakti, the Primal Power within her own being. It empowers a woman to channel her emotions in a positive direction, strengthen her weaknesses, develop mental clarity and effective communication, and give her the patience to go through the tests of her own *Karma*. It enables her to merge the limited ego into Divine Will, as well as to improve her physical health.

By practicing this meditation, a woman's thoughts, behavior, personality, and projection become aligned with the Infinite beauty and nobility unveiled by the mantra. It balances the five elements. The amazing thing is, this is such an easy meditation to do! You might pass it over because it is so simple and not realize what a profound effect it can have on your life.

Practice it faithfully, twice a day for 40 days. It is recommended for women going through menopause to practice it 5 times a day.

Best to practice on an empty stomach.

This is primarily a meditation for women, but Yogi Bhajan said that men can sit up while the woman does the meditation and silently affirm, "I am IN the Grace of God."

GOVERNING ENERGY OF EACH FINGER

Little Finger	MERCURY	Power to relate & communicate, subconscious communication with self	WATER
Ring Finger	SUN & VENUS	Physical health, vitality, grace, and beauty	FIRE
Middle Finger	SATURN	Channel emotion to devotion & patience	AIR
Index Finger	JUPITER	Wisdom and expansion, open space for change	ETHER
Thumb		Positive ego	EARTH

Meditation for Infinity, God, Purity, and Pure Power in your Navel Point (Kriya for the Third Chakra)

February 5, 1991

Time: Meditation may be done for 11 to 31 minutes. In class, it was practiced for 16 minutes.

Instructions:

1. Sit with a straight spine, chin in, chest out.

2. Hands are in Prayer Pose at the Heart Center; every part of the hand meets the other in balance. The palms and the fingers meet exactly - feel every part of the hand. Forearms are parallel to the floor.

3. Chant *Hamee Ham Brahm Ham ("Humee Hum"* by Nirinjan Kaur) using the tip of the tongue.

4. Pull in the Navel Point twice for every repetition of the mantra; pull and release the Navel lock on *Hamee Ham* and a second time on *Brahm Ham*.

5. The hands pulse like the heartbeat with the Navel lock; that is, they press together as the Navel Point is pulled in.

To End: Inhale and pull the navel up and in; press the tip of the tongue to the upper palate and concentrate. Hold for 20 seconds and exhale. Repeat twice more.

Comments:

"There is a problem: what I know nobody knows. So actually, the idea was that in my last mile of life I should leave the knowledge, for the record. You may enjoy it or not, or you are going to do it or not, that's not my problem. You know, every day I go through lots of hassles dealing with people's very difficult problems. People have their phenomena, their facets, their projections, their insecurities, and a lot of fears. That's the way this whole world is, angry and upset, because the third chakra is not balanced.... [All that is] high and low is balanced at Third Chakra - it is a point of pure energy. If you do not know how to balance the third chakra, you may have all the degrees, all the knowledge, all the money, all the beauty, but guaranteed unhappy. It is not what you feel, it is not what you know, it is not what you can do, it is how you balance it.

"... That Infinity, that God, that purity, that power, that pure power is in your Navel Point. You can't buy it, you can't sell it; and I cannot give [it to] you, and you cannot take it. But I will give you the technological knowledge through which you can initiate it so that it will start working for you. What will that mean ultimately? I am not saying that there will be no problems, I am not saying that there will be no rush, I am not saying that there will not be scandals, I am not saying anything, but you will be untouched. You can sit like a lotus, in the muddy waters, and enjoy life—that is the power of the Third Chakra."

Meditation Key to Unlock the Unlimited, Infinite Power in You

October 11, 1999

Time: 24 minutes, 2½ minutes, 2 minutes. 28½ minutes total.

Instructions:

Part One –

1. Sit in Easy Pose.

2. Place your left hand on your heart. Right upper arm is at your side, by the ribs, elbow bent and forearm extending forward parallel to the floor. Right palm faces upward and is cupped as if to receive water.

3. Inhale deeply through "O"-shaped mouth, as if drinking air. Exhale through the nose. Don't pull the air in, breathe in as if you are drinking it.

4. Continue for 22 minutes.

5. For an additional two minutes, maintain the posture and use your navel to create a powerful Breath of Fire through the "O"-mouth.

Part Two – Without stopping the breath, continue Breath of Fire through the "O"-mouth and change the hand position – left arm extends forward with the hand cupped and the right hand is on the heart. When you change the hand position, you will notice the difference. Contintue for 2½ minutes.

Part Three – Without stopping the breath, continue Breath of Fire through the "O"-mouth. Stretch both arms out to the sides, elbows straight, palms up. Continue for 2 minutes.

To End: Inhale, hold the position and hold the breath for 10-15 seconds as you stretch the spine up straight. Exhale. Repeat and exhale. Inhale again and hold the breath for 15 seconds. Stretch the extended arms from the shoulders out to the sides as far as you can. Exhale and relax.

Comments:

This exercise will stimulate your immune system and your heart muscle.

Meditation to Merge with the Infinite

February 3, 2000

Time: 11, 22, or 31 minutes.

Instructions:

1. Sit in a comfortable position.

2. Raise the right arm and hand straight up, lifting the shoulder, with the palm facing towards you, open the five fingers widespread. Left hand rests on the left knee.

3. Chant *"Sat Naam"* in a constant rhythm, about once per second. On *"Sat,"* pull the Navel Point all the way in towards the spine. On *"Naam,"* relax it. (Note: This kriya is a modified *"Sat Kriya."*)

Eyes Focus: Eyes closed.

Comments:

"We used our available sources to reach to you because I don't want to discuss things in a way that is very polite – I want to discuss the way things are going to be. We have thirteen years left to the year of the cusp.... Somebody was reminding me that in New York in 1972, we said that man is going to be dependent on one-press of a button to have all the knowledge. It is true today.

"As far as you are concerned, your problems are not what you think they are. Your problem is [that] there are certain kriyas that you have to do, and you have stopped doing them. We are based on Breath of Fire, we are based on Sat Kriya, we are based on *Saa, Taa, Naa, Maa* [Kirtan Kriya]. ... The criteria of human that you are going to face is not very progressively healthy. I am not giving you a warning, doomsday is not going to come, but you are all going to be sick. You will be... if you do not do [these kriyas].

"...If you can do Sat Kriya in different variations your chakras will be opened. And when the chakras are open, it creates a light-wavelength pressure. You go upwards. When you go upwards, this *maya,* for which you are becoming jerks, comes from all sides to lift you up. Sat Kriya for 31 minutes a day is the essence of human life."

Meditation for Power and Control of Our Own Caliber

March 13, 1979

Time: Begin by practicing for 3-4 minutes and slowly build the time. Maximum time is 11 minutes.

Instructions:

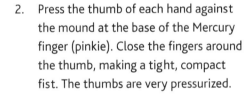

1. Sit in easy pose with a straight spine.

2. Press the thumb of each hand against the mound at the base of the Mercury finger (pinkie). Close the fingers around the thumb, making a tight, compact fist. The thumbs are very pressurized.

3. Press the fists together so that the second segments of the backs of the fingers of the right hand are touching corresponding second segments of the backs of the fingers of the left hand. The backs of the hands, from the third knuckles to the wrists, face away from each other.

4. Bend your elbows and let them rest at your sides. Place the mudra in front of the chest at the level of the heart.

Eyes Focus: Look at the tip of the nose.

Breath: Completely inhale through the nose. Exhale through the mouth. Inhale through the mouth. Exhale through the nose.

Continue rhythmically alternating the breath between the nose and the mouth in this manner. Let the breath be complete: inhale and exhale about 4 seconds in length, 8 seconds total.

To End: Inhale deeply to your maximum, hold the breath as you really stretch your spine, arms, and hands upward. Stretch as if you are trying to lift yourself off the ground. Exhale and repeat two more times.

Comments:

Caliber is the ability to maintain the projected status and activity of our command self. When we become our own directive authority, then the psyche can fulfil the self, and you can be happy. Normally, we reject authority and initiate chaos out of an attempt to create individuality by difference rather than through integrity and wholeness. This meditation enhances your capacity for caliber, to hold and execute self-authority.

"If you correctly and rhythmically practice this exercise, you will become saints. It gives power and control [of your] own caliber. It will affect the pituitary gland. You should just *do* it."

Meditation to Purify Yourself so as to be Worthy of Confronting God

July 21, 1983

Time: Not specified.

Instructions:

1. Sit in easy pose as a perfect yogi. Imagine yourself in a holy posture. This imagery is very important. In this posture, you are communicating with God. God is your concept. Imagine the image of God.

2. Imagine you are telling God: *Dukh Bhanjan Tera Naam ji. Dukh Bhanjan Tera Naam.*

   "Thy Name takes away our pain, harassment and negativity." – Guru Arjan Dev ji, *Siri Guru Granth Sahib*, page 218.

3. Listen to the *shabad*, "*Dukh Bhanjan Tera Naam Ji*" as you meditate.

Comments:

"It is a communication imagery.... With that *shabad*, the Guru communicated. With the same *shabad*, you communicate. Communicate in confrontation, apply your concentration, and don't be humble. It's a talk between two buddies, two friends. Consolidate yourself - face to face - the Unknown God and the known self. This is the highest imagery that has brought people an experience which cannot be explained. Understand the rules, and then you must act. Bring yourself together as worthy and as competent as God.... Sit in a very meditative posture. Purify yourself [to be] worthy to confront Almighty God. Self and God - let them come face to face. Now communicate through Guru's Word exactly as it comes to you."

Meditation to Recognize the Self, Infinity Will Serve that Person

April 4, 1972

Time: 11 minutes.

Instructions:

1. Sit in Easy Pose with a straight spine.

2. Make the right hand into a fist with the thumb extended. Grasp the fist with the left hand. This is known as a *kumbh*. Press this *kumbh*, the right thumb, into the Navel Point.

3. Begin long, deep, and slow breathing. Concentrate on the flow of the breath between the Navel Point and the root of the nose.

4. The breath has to be measured from the root of the nose to belly as you inhale and belly to the root of the nose when you exhale. This measurement is your meditation and if your mind expands to a limitless Infinity, enjoy it, don't break it.

Eyes Focus: Close your eyes and concentrate at the root of the nose.

To End: At the end of the meditation, inhale deeply, exhale, and relax.

Comments:

"If the body does not sustain you, get over it. Sometimes the energy in this is released so much that the mind gets scattered and you feel like not doing it. This experience [tells you] that you are [doing it] right. Within a small time, the mind will get scattered. That's the first sign. Cross that and you will find a relaxation. After that, you will find that you are entering a stage of no bounds, no limits, a floating stage. Develop [beyond] that and you will experience what you want to experience.

Keep the spine straight. Inhale deep, and when you reach the navel point, feel the *Satya* there and exhale and feel the *Naam,* and measure the breath in that length. And also start measuring the Universe within and without. Fifteen pounds to twenty pounds pressure per inch square is what is essential."

Meditation to Take Care of Ego Problem and Live as the Image of God

March 2, 1977

Time: Not Specified

Instructions:

1. Sit in a comfortable meditative posture with a straight spine.

2. Press the thumbs into the armpits. Curl the fingers down onto the mounds of the hands and rest the hands against the chest. Elbows are relaxed down.

3. Inhale deeply and then exhale completely as the mantra is chanted aloud in a monotone voice. One repetition takes approximately 10 seconds.

Eyes Focus: 1/10th open.

Mantra:

Gobinday Mukanday Udaaray Apaaray

Hareeang Kareeang Nirnaamay Akaamay[3]

---

3   From the *Jaap Sahib* by Guru Gobind Singh ji.

Comments:

"The body position must be perfect in order to derive the maximum benefits from this meditation. It is true that God's Name can make you divine, but it is also true that you should have body, mind, and spirit in the meditation so that you can practice it correctly.

"All mudras are meant to control the activity of the brain, the flow of energy and the control of your psyche. If you understand these three, then these fingers are very important. In simple language, these fingers can create very beautiful [sound from the] piano.

"It requires training. It's a very perfect posture and most painful. These thumbs go right into the armpit, hands go on the side. The body is clean and clear."

Meditation to Take the Finite to Infinity

October 2, 1972

Time: 11 minutes.

Instructions:

1. Sit in Easy Pose with a straight spine.

2. Place the hands in *Gyan Mudra*.

3. Raise the arms parallel to the floor and bend the elbows at 90 degrees with the hands point straight up.

4. Slowly and rhythmically chant the mantra *Whaa-hay Guroo,* breaking it into 4 distinct sounds as in *Laya Yoga* - *"Whaa-Hay-Gur-Roo."*

Eyes Focus: Close your eyes and concentrate on the Third Eye, the point between the eyebrows at the root of the nose.

Comments:

In every question (*Gur*) there is an answer (*Roo*). *Whaa* is the Infinite that encompasses both. It is through practicing meditations such as this one that you will gain the experience and capacity to go into deep meditative consciousness. Use this experience and time to fully explore the infinity at the center of neutrality.

"[When} a man breaks the atom, he creates a huge energy; that is what mantra yoga, *Laya Yoga,* does. And [when] a man breaks the sound and vibrates it, it creates a tremendous energy."

Meditation to Tune Vagus Nerve to Cosmic Consciousness

September 7, 1978

Time: Both mantras can be chanted for 3 to 11 minutes.

Instructions:

1. Sit in easy pose with a straight spine.

2. Relax the arms down with the elbows bent. Interlace the fingers and thumbs in a tight lock in front of the Heart Center. Keep a tight pressure on the lock.

3. With the hands joined in a tightly held fist, neutralize the energy. Attend to how you feel and observe that you automatically start to feel great. The harder you press and the stronger you make this two-handed fist, the greater you feel.

4. Chant *Ong Kaar*. Chant evenly in a 3-beat rhythm: *Ong* (one) *Kaar* (two-three) without pausing for a full breath.

5. Continue chanting *Ong Kaar*, breathing as needed to maintain a steady rhythm.

6. Continue the position and chant *Eik Ong Kaar*. Chanting evenly in a 4-beat rhythm: *Eik* (one), Ong (two), *Kaar* (three-four) without pausing for a full breath.

7. Continue chanting *Eik Ong Kaar*, breathing as needed to maintain a steady rhythm.

To End: Inhale deeply, exhale and relax.

Comments:

"The harder you press and the stronger the fist you make, you will automatically create a feeling that you are great. When chanting *Ong Kaar*, do not touch the tongue to the upper palate, ...[you want the] pressure to be so subtle, created by the air only. This is one mantra in which you do not touch the tongue to the upper palate at all. Unless the mantras are pronounced properly, the proper stimulation in the brain and mind due to air pressure on the upper palate will not be achieved, and the desired results will not be complete.

Eik is the Infinite Light. *Ong Kaar* is the vehicle that carries everything, the Infinite Light and creativity of God. *Ong Kaar* is the stimulus of the magnetic field of the cosmic consciousness into the definite finite one. Chanting *Eik Ong Kaar* tunes the vagus nerve, which in turn tunes everything around and within."

Japa

You know *Japa* is when you sit and meditate on a mantra. And you spend days and days and days and days in constant repetition of God and that eliminates the ego. It milds the ego, milds the ego. More the ego is mild, [more] your finite infinity starts seeing the Infinite Infinity. First you do things to be secure on the earth, then you start seeing things beyond the earth. And that which is called "beyond earth" is what higher consciousness is. When you start seeing that, you become humble because when you see a greatness you become humble. So when you see the creativity of the Creator and you compare that with yourself as a creature, you start seeing the vastness and the happiness. That is how the consciousness becomes happy. And [to experience] this, we chant the *Japa*.

August 17, 1976

Defeat can be eaten up by *Japa*, because *Japa* is the repetition of that holy *Nam*, the Naad that connects you with God. it's an area code number of the Lord God, the Infinity. It's a *Japa*. *Japa* creates *Tapa*. *Tapa* means the heat which burns up the *Karma*. When *Karma* gets burnt up, then you get to *Dharma*. When you get *Dharma*, it's a path to God.

November 6, 1976

Japa is a science and when you create this sound in a *Japa*, then it brings the power of God to you.

August 10, 1982

What is *Japa*? *Japa* is repeating the Name of God. It didn't say it should be just one word. It didn't say it should be eight words. It didn't say it can be millions of words and it can be totally no word. I just want to tell you a very simple thing in body language. This (index) finger, when you raise it, it tells where God is. And I am not going to raise the second (middle) finger, but if I raised it you would all get up and ask me what the hell I am doing. Just as raising the wrong finger can mess me up, speaking the wrong word can mess you up. Because power of the word is not limited. Wrong word can damage you, just like God, and right word can elevate you, just like God.

July 31, 1983

Japa means repeating and praising the Lord.

July 31, 1983

Japa gives *Tapa*. When you repeat the Name of God it creates a special heat, it is called *Tapa*. That burns the *Karma* and that gives you the *Dharma*. It's a simple known law.

July 31, 1983

"In the beginning there was the Word and word was with God and word was God."[1] If that is true and that is what Guru Nanak, the Guru, said.

ਅਖਰੀ ਨਾਮੁ ਅਖਰੀ ਸਾਲਾਹ

ਅਖਰੀ ਗਿਆਨੁ ਗੀਤ ਗੁਣ ਗਾਹ

ਅਖਰੀ ਲਿਖਣੁ ਬੋਲਣੁ ਬਾਣਿ

ਅਖਰਾ ਸਿਰਿ ਸੰਜੋਗੁ ਵਖਾਣਿ

Akhree Nam, akhree salah

akhree gyan geeth gunn ga,

akhree likhan bolan bann

akra seer sanjog vikaan.[2]

Siri Guru Granth Sahib

---

1 The Holy Bible, Genisis 1:1

2 Guru Nanak Dev ji, Japji Sahib

All your destiny is written in word. So if you speak God's word, if you speak divine words, those words will rewrite the destiny if it is wrong.

July 31, 1983

I will tell you something – this is what it is, take it or leave it: God gave you health, wealth, and happiness. If you do not dedicate back towards God, you will create a separation. That is what *Japa* is about. *Ja-Pa* – there are two words in it. *Ja* means "go", *Pa* means "get". Go and get.

July 23, 1987

Japa creates *Tapa*. *Tapa* is the heat that purifies… *Japa* means the recitation and that creates *Tapa*, the heat. Heat burns the *Karma* and then born is the *Dharma*. And when *Dharma* is born, then kindness and compassion rule. When *Dharma* is born, kindness and compassion rule and under that rule God dwells. *Japa* creates the *Tapa*, *Tapa* burns the *Karma* and that burnt *Karma* ,that mulch, creates the *Dharma*. And in that *Dharma*, there is a rule of kindness and compassion in which God dwells.

July 30, 1987

Aad Sach, Jugaad Sach
Hai Bhee Sach, Nanak Hosee Bhee Sach

ਆਦਿ ਸਚੁ ਜੁਗਾਦਿ ਸਚੁ ॥
ਹੈ ਭੀ ਸਚੁ ਨਾਨਕ ਹੋਸੀ ਭੀ ਸਚੁ ॥੧॥

Siri Guru Granth Sahib[3]

There is only one commandment, look at the beauty of the *Siri Guru Granth*, look at this most beautiful, wonderful line. There is only one commandment in *Siri Guru Granth*. It says, 'repeat it;' repeat it as many time as you can repeat it. And what to repeat? What to remember? What to be?

Aad Sach, Jugaad Sach, Hai Bhee Sach, Nanak Hosee Bhee Sach.
Sabh Gobind Hai, Sabh Gobind Hai, Gobind Bin Nahe Koe[4]

You will not understand it if you do not give value to the truth; you will not give value to the depth of that truth; you will not give value to truth-depth within you. You will not even understand happiness in life, if you do not understand the happiness in you and your soul. Dance with your soul, get to it; you will relate to it, you will be a realized person. And when everybody realizes you are a realized person, then life starts.

January 27, 1991

---

3   Guru Nanak Dev ji, Japji Sahib

4   Siri Guru Granth Sahib, Bhagat Naam Dev ji, page 485

The communion, the *Japa*, know you, know I know *Jap*, what?

Aad Sach, Jugaad Sach, Hai Bhee Sach, Nanak Hosee Bhee Sach.

This total thing is known as *Mool Mantra*. That's why, it's possible for a man to meditate and say, "God and me, and me and God are one"– as bubble and ocean, ocean and bubble, are one because the root is one. That's it.

November 15, 1975

The *Akaal Takhat*, is *Akaal Sahay*, the Infinite shall serve you, will protect you, will come through when a finite is encircled by Infinity, which every finite is. Each, even the atom, has its own orbit, its own impulse. Now, human has the aura, but basically, we are lonely. God is and it is. Our purpose is to repeat it. That's why Guru Nanak said,

Aad Sach, Jugaad Sach, Hai Bhee Sach, Nanak Hosee Bhee Sach.

Those who have found *sach*, their life shall be away from the *kach*, – falsehood shall not come near [them].

March 6, 1989

You must understand one thing in your life – Without self-respect and dignity you can never find the truth. And without truth, you can never find God. Because God is truth,

Aad Sach, Jugaad Sach, Hai Bhee Sach, Nanak Hosee Bhee Sach.

God shall always be true.

January 1, 1983

Ang Sang Whaa-hay Guroo

Ang Sang Whaa-hay Guroo

You are thirty trillions living Gods & unconscious habits are destroyed.

God made you in his own image. God dwells in you and around you and the only one line you have to remember is,

Ang Sang Whaa-hay Guroo

"With every limb, with every molecule, God is". Each one of you carry thirty trillion alive cells. Thirty trillion living gods all within each person.

July 10, 1998

Actually the words *Ang Sang Whaa-hay Guroo* is meant for destroying unconscious habits and unconscious thoughts, for which we are not willing to go through the consequences. You must remember please, thoughts shall start the sequence. That we can stop. We can destroy the thought in the subconscious and unconscious, wherever we can find it. If it's unconscious, you have to bring it into the subconscious and then strike it with the positive-triplex-mirror-three-headed missile, *Ang Sang Whaa-hay Guroo*. There are six sounds in it. It's amazing. Don't worry what it means, it doesn't worry what it is. Just do it as a penetrating therapy. That means you can penetrate yourself if you want in your subconscious and unconscious. ... [Chant] where the air joins the throat? It is right there.

July 2, 1990

Just remember you have your soul, you have your strength, you have thirty trillions living gods actively dancing in your one physical being. Now, how many gods do you want to search? That's what those words, *Ang Sang Whaa-hay Guroo* means. *Ang Sang Whaa-hay Guroo* means in Naad, in vibration, in musical sense, that you are thirty trillions living gods. Now, that's the affirmation and you are searching for one God.

September 22, 1991

God and Me, Me and God Are One

You know, we chant that mantra, "God and me, me and God are one."
It is that ecstasy of consciousness when you feel the oneness with the One,
when you feel the grace with the One, and One is all and all is One.

October 11, 1973

Har

Har is a *Shakti* Yog Mantra. *Har* is the original God. And sometimes if you chant
with me just that word *Har*, you will realize God just in couple of seconds.

January 14, 1989

Har Har Har Har Har Har Gobinday

When you want the entire universe to be in you and around you in the most
positive way, then you say,

Har Har Har Har Har Har Gobinday
Har Har Har Har Har Har Mukhanday
Har Har Har Har Har Har Udaray
Har Har Har Har Har Har Aparay
Har Har Har Har Har Har Hariang
Har Har Har Har Har Har Kariang
Har Har Har Har Har Har NirNamay
Har Har Har Har Har Har Akamay

It becomes seven words and the Infinity will serve you.

December 31, 1985

Ong Namo Guru Dev Namo

Before we start a class, we always bow to Him. *Ong*—the creative one; *Namo*—we bow, to do salutation; *Guru*—the infinite wisdom; *Dev*—the transparent that we do not see; *Namo*—salutation. *Ong Namo Guru Dev Namo* means, O Lord Creator, the infinite teacher who is transparent and unseen, I bow to Thee. Period.

October 14, 1971

Whenever you chant *Ong Namo Guru Dev Namo*, *Bhagautee*, the creative power of the universe, the manifestation of *Shakti*, of *Bhagawaan*, the God, the Ultimate, the Infinite, through the grace and blessing of *Guru Ram Das*, dwells in you as a yogi. And that is what you teach.

August 22, 1978

When you teach and call on God and Guru [by chanting] *Ong Namo Guru Dev Namo*, that is all you have to do. Then God comes through.

December 6, 1997

Sat Naam

Whosoever lives in the finite consciousness surmounts the finite by the power of his own Infinity. That is why we chant *Sat Naam* so that we relate to that Infinity.

January 23, 1975

When you are disturbed, and when you want to bring to yourself the peace and oneness of God but you are not in a position to do anything, then we announce, speak, or utter, or create the Panch Shabad, five primal sounds.

Inhale deep, *Saaaaaaaat Naam*.

Now when you create the sound *sa* – *Sa* is the sound of the creativity of God. *Ta* is when you come to the end of it and the tongue and the upper palate meet, it creates the sound ta automatically. So *sa* and that makes the *ta* and then very politely and very slowly you say *Naam*. It means "God is truth" – that's what literally it means.

August 10, 1982

Acknowledgements

I am grateful to God and Guru for the opportunity to be on this path. Filled with everlasting love and gratitude, I honor Yogi Bhajan as my teacher and guide. I also deeply respect and am thankful for Guru Dev Singh, the master of *Sat Nam Rasayan*®, who has deepened my awareness, understanding, and experience of Yogi Ji's teachings and of life. *Sat Nam Rasayan* is an ancient healing path taught by Yogi Bhajan, which allows the practitioner to foster growth in consciousness. Thank you to the Kundalini Research Institute® (KRI) and its many donors for the Yogi Bhajan Library of Teachings® (the collected audio, video, transcribed lectures, and meditations and kriyas of Yogi Bhajan: libraryofteachings.com). Special thanks to Shanti Kaur Khalsa for your artful editing contributions, to Ditta Khalsa for coordinating our efforts so beautifully, and to the KRI publishing team.

Glossary

Aad Sach, Jugaad Sach, Hai Bhee Sach, Naanak Hosee Bhee Sach: It is the highest prayer. In the beginning, he was true; through the time, he's true; now, he's true and Nanak, he shall always be true. 5/11/78

Ajoonee, Saibhang: never born, never die, by itself. 7/14/89

Akaal Takhat: Takhat of the Akaal, the throne of the undying superiority of the Infinite. 1/26/75 Akaal Takhat remind us that we are a part of infinity, we are a part of reality, we are the infinite. 6/6/90

Ang Sang Whaa-hay Guroo: God is with my every limb. 6/24/79 With each limb of mine, with each part of me, God lives. 10/15/79

Apana eliminates what does not allow the life to be contained. 12/20/74

Aquarian Age: The Piscean Age is I want to know, take me there. The Aquarian Age I want the experience, give me. 8/29/97 The great mantra of the Age of Aquarius is keep up. 1/10/77 This Aquarian age is 'I know,' Piscean Age is 'I want to know.' 11/18/91

Avagavan, coming and going 6/24/79

Avatar: No liberation out of the Tattvas can be available, can be available without the human body. That's why Almighty God when has to perform a conscious act then He takes over the human body, that's called incarnation or Avatar. 8/26/77

Bana is not that just white clothes you wear and you look like a nun or you belong to some Christian order and all that stuff, that's not true. Bana has one projection, bana is connected what you want to project. Bana multiplies your meditative identify. 7/8/81

Bani is a cosmic power contained in the permutation and combination of that naad, originated by the Gurus, and which is contained in the living vibratory essence, the Siri Guru Granth Sahib. 8/14/78

Bhagautee, the creative power of the universe 8/22/78

Bhagawaan, the God, the Ultimate, the Infinite 8/22/78

Gurbani means Guru's word 2/28/77

Gurmukhi means mouth of the Guru. This language was branded as Gurmukhi, the language of the Guru. Why? It was the need of the time. Because you always require a middleman to translate the scripture. 9/22/75

Guru Nanak taught something, that at time your existence still belong to the non-existence. Guru Nanak was the first Guru of the Udaasi panth and that was that you have to be unattached while living, working and being in everything. 11/18/94 The basic teaching of Guru Nanak is that you are by grace, you are by virtue, you are by blessing, time doesn't exist, time only makes you to appear. So you have come from Akaal Purakh, as Akaal Moorat, go through the time as Akaal Moorat and merge in Akaal Purakh as Akaal Moorat, that is exactly what Guru Nanak said. 11/18/94

Har is the original God 1/14/89 Har is the creative sound of the conscious mind, and it has to be created between the upper palate and the tip of the tongue and the force must come from the navel. 4/16/83

Jap means repeat. That means Sikh has no right to give up, truth must be repeated again and again and again and again and again. 6/10/96

Japa is repeating the name of God. 7/31/83 Your effectiveness is what you speak. And your trust is what you speak and deliver. And your respect and goodwill is you deliver again and again and again, it's called Japa. Japa means Jee-Paa, Paa means get, Jee means the soul. Get to the soul. Repeat it, repeat it, repeat it to get to the soul. 7/20/88

Khalsa exactly means, purest of the pure. 6/28/91

Meditation is when you can extend yourself into infinity for all the relevant vibrations around you. It's an action of polarity. It's a totality of truth. 5/18/74 What's meditation? To clean the subconscious. Every garbage. 12/6/88

Naad means the sound current, the balance and imbalance of the sound current. 7/5/78 What is a naad? Vibratory interaction. 7/10/75

Naam (also Nam). Word Naam means totality. Word Naam means identity. 3/7/92 Naam means the sound of the infinite. 4/20/75

Nimith is for the sake of 6/24/79

Nirbho Nirvair. You have to be without fear and you have to be without vengeance. 12/23/87

Nith means you live for your own sake 6/24/79 Nith means everyday affair shall be taken care of 2/7/88

Prakirti: prakirti means the woman. All of you are prakirti, all men, women, animals, birds. Eight point four million life span and their household and everything is nothing but prakirti. Everything, which is born or dead exists in time and space is called creation, prakirti. It is a female, gender wise and one, which never dies and never is born is called purkha it is a male. 8/4/80

Prana is what comes in your life through the breath. We call it breath of life. 11/23/76

Purkha: See Prakirti

Sach khand means the realm of truth. 7/22/77

Sadhana is when you come, you are told the discipline as we have given Sadhana. Get up this morning, take bath, do this. That is a Sadhana. It is not a way. It is not a religion. What is it? It is a technology. It is Gur. 7/20/78 It is to know your soul, it is know your God, it is to experience and merge in it which is dormant. And what is sadhana? A complete systematic system in which man physically mentally and spiritually participated, participates and will be participating tomorrow within the concept of God. 3/18/83

Samskara are the impressions of the previous life which the mental body carries along with it when it takes the soul from the body to a distant land. ... It's a previous relationship which has come to settle the account. 12/9/79

Satya means true energy, real energy, the infinite energy. God of God of God of God. 7/3/88

Seva when you serve another person. 9/9/90 Seva means service without price. 7/16/81 Seva, selfless service, to solve other people's problem and pain. 8/11/91

Shabad, the word, is the total power of God. 10/14/85 The shabad is that cuts down that badhi, that bad luck 11/1/92

Simran: The meditative repetition of the Holy Naam is called Simran. 7/16/80 Continuously you hear the mantra, and continuously you remember that the mantra. 7/4/77 Simran means only repeatingly meditate. Jap and Simran are two different things. Jap is repeated for the hypothalamus. Simran is repeated for the frontal lobe, which controls the personality of a human being. 2/8/94

Siri Guru Granth: There are eighty-four meridian points on the upper palate of every human being. The ling is the tongue, and when you read the Siri Guru Granth the tongue rotates on those meridian points making the thalamus to secrete, giving an ecstasy of consciousness to the man who reads it. 9/17/76 The essence of ten masters and other holy men who have reached to God in the state of consciousness and their Bani, their words, which only come according to the science of knowledge perfect[ed] to be honored as Siri Guru Granth have been [in] the Siri Guru Granth. Therefore, meditating on Shabad or reading the Siri Guru Granth keeps you...to reach the state of consciousness. 12/10/78

Tattvas: There are five different specific frequency ranges of pranic vibrations, each associated with a different chakra. These frequency ranges are known as tattvas or basic 'elements' and are designated as: earth, water, fire, air, and ether. We can most readily experience them as emotions, but they serve other energy functions in the body as well. 4/25/88

Vayus: Breath of life is the base, is the cornerstone on which the life lives but breath of life has five more airs, vayu they call them. 2/12/86

Resources

The Kundalini Research Institute

Your Source for Kundalini Yoga as Taught by Yogi Bhajan®
Teacher Training, Online Resources, Publishing, and Research

www.kundaliniresearchinstitute.org

The Yogi Bhajan Library of Teachings

Keeping the Legacy Alive!

www.libraryofteachings.com

3HO - Healthy Happy Holy Organization

For information regarding international events:

www.3HO.org

To find a teacher in your area or for more information
about becoming a Kundalini Yoga teacher:

www.kundaliniyoga.com

For more information about mantras and music
used with these meditations:

www.kundaliniresearchinstitute.org

www.spiritvoyage.com

iTunes or CDBaby.com

About Hargopal Kaur Khalsa

Hargopal Kaur Khalsa worked in the aerospace industry for many years and now devotes her time to teaching Sat *Nam* Rasayan®, yoga, and meditation; facilitating family constellations; and serving clients. Her passion is to uplift and help people, enabling them to grow and feel better emotionally, physically, mentally, and spiritually. Through her own meditative practice and studies with Yogi Bhajan, Guru Dev Singh, and Bert Hellinger, she raises her vibration in order to serve clearly, neutrally, and compassionately. Hargopal is based in Los Angeles and travels in the US, Canada, and Europe to teach and see clients. She has compiled and edited several other books based on Yogi Bhajan's teachings and intends to continue this joyful process.